365 Travel

365 Travel

A Daily Book of Journeys,
Meditations,
and Adventures

EDITED BY LISA BACH

TRAVELERS' TALES
SAN FRANCISCO

Travelers' Tales and Travelers' Tales Guides are trademarks of Travelers' Tales, Inc., 330 Townsend Street, Suite 208, San Francisco, California 94107. www.travelerstales.com

Credits and copyright notices are given starting on page 367.

Art Direction and design: Michele Wetherbee
Illustration: © Leigh Wells
Interior Design: Melanie Haage
Page Layout: Melanie Haage, using the fonts Bulmer and Medici Script

Distributed by: Publishers Group West, 1700 Fourth Street, Berkeley, California 94710.

Library of Congress Cataloging-in-Publication Data
365 travel: a daily book of journeys, meditations, and adventures /
edited by Lisa Bach.—1st ed.
    p. cm.
        ISBN 1-885211-67-8
Travel—Quotations, maxims, etc. I. Title: Three hundred sixty-
five travel. II Bach, Lisa, 1968-

PN6084.T7 A15 2001
910—dc21   2001025003

First Printing
Printed in the United States of America
10 9 8 7 6 5 4 3 2 1

The world is a book, and those who do not travel,
read only a page.

—SAINT AUGUSTINE (354–430)
The City of God

INTRODUCTION

I could travel every day of the year. Waking up exhilarated in a new unexplored city; finding a restaurant known only to locals; starting a conversation with someone simply to share a common connection; having no plan for the day except to possibly get lost and find the real essence of the place. These are only a few of the reasons that I yearn to travel. There is something about taking a journey—crossing and expanding both geographical and personal boundaries—that has ingrained itself so completely in me that it can never fully be sated. So what's my antidote for not being on the road all the time? I open a book to soothe my wanderlust.

And yet I almost never read while traveling. Most people use their vacations and trips to catch up on the latest novel or book that's been collecting dust on the nightstand. While on a three-month solo journey through Europe a couple of years ago, I couldn't bring myself to read a book. Was this something to worry about? As an editor, avid reader, and collector of books, I felt as if I'd been stricken with a fatal disease. A book couldn't sustain my attention for more than a page, let alone a chapter or the full book. Other travelers were exchanging paperbacks—no one dare carry a hardcover—but the book I brought with me for the plane ride over stayed with me for the entire trip. Was it the book or me? I searched out English language bookstores to try to find another book, and the travelers to whom I explained my dilemma tried to convince me their latest read would surely hold my attention. But nothing worked.

Then on the AVE high-speed train from Madrid to Seville, all alone in a train car with a Spanish-dubbed version of Goldie Hawn's *Overboard* playing, I finally realized what was happening. I had enjoyed so many other travel narratives that I was terrified of missing my own. I didn't want to miss the breadth of landscape as it changed outside my train window. I didn't want to miss an opportunity of meeting someone new. I didn't want to get lost in a book. I wanted to revel in my journey. And the only way to do that was to be present and conscious on my trip. I still had the desire to read but only short passages that would inspire me on the journey I was on. I didn't need the full narrative.

This explains in part the genesis of *365 Travel,* a book that is an essential companion—a talisman to turn to day or night to find comfort, wisdom, and inspiration, whether at home or on the road. We all have snapshots in our photo albums and images that linger in our minds of trips we've taken. When something sparks a travel memory in you—the sun on the drive home reminds you of the light slanting over a vineyard in Tuscany; the smell of curry in your kitchen takes you back to an extraordinary meal you had in New Delhi; you stumble and remember the vertigo you felt after climbing to the top of the Pyramid of Kukulcan of Chichen Itzá in the Yucatan—you have a brief glimpse of the many reasons you are passionate about travel.

From well-known travel writers to everyday travelers, the passages collected in *365 Travel* give you the full spectrum of travel experiences, as well as evocative portraits of places all over the world. Harriet Martineau describes what a sunset in Egypt was like in 1848. Kathleen Norris reveals the spiritual geography of North Dakota. Alex Shoumatoff paints the Southwest as an old sea floor. Mary Morris uncovers how you know when you are officially addicted to travel. And Frances Mayes tells how memory can be a trickster that only keeping a travel journal can help outwit. There are hundreds of other adventures and observations that will remind you of your own travel experiences, teach you a tip or two, open you up to fully experience the world around you, or perhaps encourage and inspire you to plan your next journey.

365 Travel provides you with travel wisdom for every day of the year. Throughout my reading and research, I was astonished by the diversity and the extent of literature available. I encourage you to refer to the acknowledgments at the end of the book and to use it as a roadmap through the rich and varied literary travel landscape. And remember, each day offers you a journey without ever leaving your home. Your imagination is your ticket to the world, and *365 Travel* can be your inspiration.

WHERE IN THE WORLD?

*W*HERE COULD EVERYBODY BE, I WONDERED. HOW still it was in this old, old city of Paris in the first hour of the New Year.

The year before, I had been in Cleveland. The year before that in San Francisco. The year before that in Mexico City. The one before that at Carmel. And the year before Carmel in Tashkent. Where would I be when the next New Year came, I wondered?

—LANGSTON HUGHES, *I Wonder as I Wander*

HOOKED ON TRAVEL

*O*NE SURE SIGN OF TRAVELERS IS THEIR RELATIONSHIP to maps. I cannot say how much of my life I spent looking at maps, but there is no map I won't stare at and study. I love to measure each detail with my thumb, to see how far I have come, how far I've yet to go. I love maps the way stamp collectors love stamps. Not for their usefulness, but rather for the sheer beauty of the object itself. I love to look at a map, even if it is a map of Mars, and figure out where I am going and how I am going to get there, what route I will take. I imagine what adventures might await me even though I know that the journey is never what we plan for; it's what happens between the lines.

—MARY MORRIS, *Nothing to Declare*

WHEN THE FAMILIAR BECOMES EXOTIC

*T*O TRAVEL ACROSS THE GLOBE SIMPLY TO LOCATE the facilities of the place one has quit would, of course, be an elaborate exercise in perversity. Only those who travel for business, and nothing more, would really wish to ask the questions addressed by Anne Tyler's Accidental Tourist: "What restaurants in Tokyo offered Sweet'n Low? Did Amsterdam have a McDonald's? Did Mexico City have a Taco Bell? Did any place in Rome serve Chef Boyardee ravioli? Other travelers hoped to discover distinctive local wines; Macon's readers searched for pasteurized and homogenized milk." Pasteurized and homogenized cultures are not what take us abroad. Yet, at the same time, many a traveler knows that the Temple of the Golden Arches and the Palace of the Burger King never seem so appealing as when one is searching for a regular meal in the back streets of Kyoto. And Father Time never seems so authoritative, or so agreeably familiar, as when one is yearning for news in the mountains of Tibet.

If the great horror of traveling is that the foreign can come to seem drearily familiar, the happy surprise of traveling is that the familiar can come to seem wondrously exotic.

—PICO IYER, *Video Night in Kathmandu*

January 4

TAKE NOTE OF TRAVEL MEMORIES

*T*HERE ARE PLACES I'VE BEEN WHICH ARE LOST TO me. When I was there, I followed the guide faithfully from site to site, putting check marks in the margins at night when I plotted my route for the next day. On my first trip to Italy, I was so excited that I made a whirlwind, whistlestop trip to five cities in two weeks. I still remember everything, the revelation of my first espresso under the arcades in Bologna, remarking that it stung my throat. Climbing every tower and soaking my blistered feet in the bidet at night. The candlelit restaurant in Florence where I first met ravioli with butter and sage. The pastries I bought to take to the room, all wrapped and tied like a present. The dark leather smell of the shoe store where I bought (inception of a lifelong predilection) my first pair of Italian shoes. Discovering Allori in a corner of the Uffizi. The room at the foot of the Spanish Steps where Keats died, and dipping my hand in the boat-shaped fountain just outside, thinking Keats had dipped his hand there. I kept no record of that trip. On later trips, I began to carry a travel journal because I realized how much I forgot over time. Memory is, of course, a trickster.

—FRANCES MAYES, *Under the Tuscan Sun*

SOUL JOURNEY

*T*HERE ARE AS MANY FORMS OF PILGRIMAGE AS THERE are proverbial roads to Rome.

There are journeys to fulfill religious obligation, journeys of thanks, journeys of curiosity, homage, and serendipity, even journeys of penance ("Say three Our Fathers, three hail Marys, and walk to Rome, my child"). All are journeys of renewal.

As pilgrims we go back to find something we lost; we return to the source to be restored, rejuvenated, revivified. I've traveled as tourist, traveler, adventure tour guide, and writer, and have been overjoyed to see things with new eyes.... But it has been as a pilgrim—to Angkor Wat, Easter Island, Chartres, Pablo Neruda's house in Valparaiso, Chile, Rumi's tomb in Konya, Turkey—that I have felt most alive. Something happened at each of these sites that vitalized me and helped clarify my deepest thoughts.

The bona fide soul journey echoes John Muir's realization at Yosemite a century ago, "I only went out for a walk, and finally concluded to stay out till sundown, for going out, I found out I was really going in."

—PHIL COUSINEAU, Introduction,
Pilgrimage: Adventures of the Spirit

January 6

Not So Foreign

ONE OF THE PARADOXES OF OTHERNESS IS THAT IN travel, each conceives the other to be a foreigner. But even the most distant and exotic place has its parallel in ordinary life. Every day we meet new people and are insulted or misunderstood; we are thrown upon our own resources. In the coming and going of daily life we rehearse a modified version of the dramatic event known as first contact. In a wish to experience otherness to its limit, to explore all its nuances, I became a traveler. I was as full of preconceived notions as Columbus or Crusoe—you can't help it, but you can alter such thoughts. Nontravelers often warn the traveler of dangers, and the traveler dismisses such fears, but the presumption of hospitality is just as odd as the presumption of danger. You have to find out for yourself. Take the leap. Go as far as you can. Try staying out of touch. Become a stranger in a strange land. Acquire humility. Learn the language. Listen to what people are saying.

—Paul Theroux, *Fresh Air Fiend*

THE ARNO

Y ROOM AT THE INN LOOKED OUT ON THE RIVER and was flooded all day with sunshine. There was an absurd orange-colored paper on the walls; the Arno, of a hue not altogether different, flowed beneath. All this brightness and yellowness was a perpetual delight; it was a part of that indefinably charming color which Florence always seems to wear as you look up and down at it from the river, and from the bridges and quays. This is the kind of grace radiance—a harmony of high tints—which I scarce know how to describe.

—HENRY JAMES, *The Italian Hours* (1909)

THE ART OF SAUNTERING

I HAVE MET WITH BUT ONE OR TWO PERSONS IN THE course of my life who understood the art of Walking, that is, of taking walks—who had a genius, so to speak,  for *sauntering*: which word is beautifully derived "from the idle people who roved about the country, in the Middle Ages, and asked charity, under pretense of going *á la Sainte Terre*," to the Holy Land, till the children exclaimed, "There goes a *Sainte-Terrer*," a Saunterer, a Holy-Lander. They who never go to the Holy Land in their walks, as they pretend, are indeed mere idlers and vagabonds; but they who do go there are saunterers in the good sense, such as I mean.

—HENRY DAVID THOREAU, *Walden*

THE WINDY CITY

*I*N CHICAGO YOU FEEL THE PRESSURE OF INFINITE surrounding plains; it's a city that fills the land; even the lake, enclosing one side, allows no escape. From time to time, at the end of a long ride by tramway, train, or elevated railroad, the buildings thin out, and it seems that the city is finally going to expire. Then it springs up again, even more vigorously; you've merely reached an old border, with new neighborhoods built beyond. And beyond that there's yet another belt, and another farther on. But it's not only these exorbitant dimensions that give Chicago its density. Los Angeles is vast but porous. This town is made of a thick dough, without leavening. More than any city in the world, it reeks of humanity, and this is what makes its atmosphere so stifling and tragic. Neither nature nor the past can penetrate it, but in the absence of the picturesque, it possesses a dark poetry.

—SIMONE DE BEAUVOIR, *America Day by Day*

January 10

EUPHRATES

*W*E WERE OFF EARLY THE NEXT DAY AND WENT UP river to Qulat Sahib—it was a delicious warm day and the river was delightful. I don't know why it should be as attractive as it is. The elements of the scene are extremely simple but the combination still makes a wonderfully attractive result. Yet there's really nothing—flat, far-stretching plain coming down to the river's edge, thorn-covered, water-covered in the flood in the lower reaches, a little wheat and millet stubble in the base fields, an occasional village of reed-built houses and the beautiful river craft, majestic on noble sails or skimming on clumsy paddles. The river bends and winds, curves back on itself almost and you have the curious apparition of a fleet of white sails rising out of the thorny waste, now on one side of you, now the other. And by these you mark where your cruise must be, where the river divides wilderness from wilderness.

—GERTRUDE BELL, LETTER TO HER FAMILY (1917)

MEMORY

AT LAST THE TIME CAME. DAD WOKE US UP AT 1:00 A.M., tucked us into the back of the Volkswagen bus, and we drove all night. Erich and I tried to prove how big we were by staying awake, but by the time we reached Rye, New York, we were both snoring. I do remember waking up at about 4:00 A.M. when Dad stopped for gas and got his thermos filled with coffee. The smell of coffee in the middle of the night in a car on the highway, somewhere in a part of the country I'd never been to before, made me feel like one of the astronauts on his way to the moon.

—MARK SALZMAN, *Lost in Place*

A PICNIC IN PROVENCE

*T*HE MILES OF ARCHES OF THE CONNECTING CANAL marching across the countryside provide other benefits. On another day, Bob and I were on our way to the Pont du Gard with a picnic lunch when Bob noticed a sign to the Pont Rou. Turning off D227, we came to a little circle that seemed to be in the middle of nowhere, followed the road just a little farther, and parked. Across a field was a row of Roman arches. Happily, the wind that was blowing that day was not the unpredictable mistral, but a delicious breeze filled with the aroma of wild rosemary and thyme. We spread our blanket on top of one of the arches. I don't know if it was the scent of wild spices, the feel of the ancient bridge, the wonderful pâtés, salads, cheeses, bread, and Rhône wine we had purchased, or the wild loneliness of the place—but it was the most perfect spot for a picnic.

—INA CARO, *The Road from the Past*

January 13

INDIA

*T*HIS IS INDEED INDIA! THE LAND OF DREAMS AND romance, of fabulous wealth and fabulous poverty, of splendour and rags, of palaces and hovels, of famine and pestilence, of genii and giants and Aladdin lamps, of tigers and elephants, the cobra and the jungle, the country of a hundred nations and a hundred tongues, of a thousand religions and two million gods, cradle of the human race, birthplace of human speech, mother of history, grandmother of legend, great-grandmother of Tradition, whose yesterdays bear date with the mouldering antiquities of the rest of the nations—the one sole country under the sun that is endowed with an imperishable interest for alien prince and alien peasant, for lettered and ignorant, wise and fool, rich and poor, bond and free, the one land that all men desire to see, and having seen once, by even a glimpse, would not give that glimpse for the shows of all the rest of the globe combined.

—MARK TWAIN, *More Tramps Abroad* (1897)

January 14

A Bond Between Strangers

I AGAIN STOPPED TO GREET HIM. HE SMILED AND appeared glad to see me. We spoke easily now; he in his broken English, and I in my fractured Nepali. Out of respect I now called him *daju*, or "older brother," as is the custom. The first time I addressed him as *daju* his expression did not change, but from then on he called me *bhai*, or "younger brother," as though he had been doing so for years.

I cannot explain the feeling, but there has always been something exquisitely heartwarming about being referred to as *bhai* or *daju* by the Nepalis. Perhaps these words were intended to convey nothing more than simple courtesy to a foreigner, but countless times I have been struck by the intimacy these words implied, and the genuine affection with which they were spoken.

—ROBERT J. MATTHEWS, "A SIMPLE TOUCH,"
The Gift of Travel

AN HISTORICAL ADVENTURE

COMMANDER PEARY GAVE THE WORD, "WE WILL plant the stars and stripes—*at the North Pole!*" and it was done; on the peak of a huge paleocrystic floeberg, the glorious banner was unfurled to the breeze, and as it snapped and crackled with the wind, I felt a savage joy and exultation. Another world's accomplishment was done and finished, and as in the past, from the beginning of history, wherever the world's work was done by a white man, he had been accompanied by a colored man. From the building of the pyramids and the journey to the Cross, to the discovery of the new world and the discovery of the North Pole, the Negro had been the faithful and constant companion of the Caucasian, and I felt all that it was possible for me to feel, that it was I, a lowly member of my race, who had been chosen by fate to represent it, at this, almost the last of the world's great *work*.

—MATTHEW A. HENSON,
A Negro Explorer at the North Pole (1912)

POWER CIRCLES IN BEIJING

*B*efore sunrise, as the smog-tinged haze thins from the city, the public gardens fill with students, factory workers, old men, women in slippers and hairnets, all bent on *taijiquan*, "ultimate supreme boxing." Along every path and clearing their arms and legs lift and rotate in grace shadow-play, while the faces above them look closed away. The motions of the most expert unfurl in a rhythmic flow. Their breath comes steady and deep. Their gaze follows their elbows or fingertips. In another country they would be taken for mad. Whereas Western calisthenics are charged and strenuous, *taijiquan* looks more like the sloweddown film of a lost martial art. Its aim is not to turn the body more slim or dynamic, but more flexible and poised. In it, the national mind seems to be concentrated for the day ahead, as if the people were in training for a subtle passive resistance. Self is achieving equilibrium.

—COLIN THUBRON, *Behind the Wall*

SEEING LIFE ANEW

*T*HEN IT WAS SPRINGTIME IN THE CLOUDY HIMALAYAS. Nine hundred feet below my cave rhododendrons blossomed. I climbed barren mountaintops. Long tramps led me to desolate valleys studded with translucent lakes…. Solitude, solitude!… Mind and senses develop their sensibility in this contemplative life made up of continual observations and reflections. Does one become a visionary or, rather, is it not that one has been blind until then?

—ALEXANDRA DAVID-NEEL,
Magic and Mystery in Tibet (1931)

Your Spirit Soars

A SMALL PLANE IS PURE MAGIC. THE RUNWAY SKIMS by, the engine screaming in anticipation, the nose lifts, the seat springs groan and creak as your body weight doubles in the first thrust of flight, and—you're off. The ground drops away, becoming a rinky-dink, toy-town picture book of dollhouses and Matchbox cars and spongy trees and tiny white-spired churches.

The world is all yours. You can go anywhere, do anything, turn left, turn right, fly in circles, climb, dive, do a somersault, loop-a-loop if you must, play peek-a-boo with clouds, chase a rainbow, tease a thunderhead, skim a spuming surf, kiss a mountain top, make the long grasses wave like silky hair, roll your wings at a farmer in his field, bombard the cumulus galleons with their wind-ripped sails. Your spirit soars with the plane; you feel light as duck down, free as a feather. And you remember, you know again, just how precious and perfect life and being alive can be. The high of the whole. The best high of all. Because it's true.

—DAVID YEADON, *The Way of the Wanderer*

ONE OF THE SUPREME SIGHTS OF THE ANDES

YOU JOURNEY TO MACHU PICCHU—SOME FIFTY MILES north of Cuzco—by rail, through high and flowering valleys of broom. Then the mountains close in, the corridors of the gorges begin. You shiver at ten thousand feet and stare at the sky for a sight of the condor that never comes; you drop down into the dripping tropical forest that clots the air. The mountains shut you in. The train whistle sends echoes bounding from wall to wall; outside their huts, the Indians stand, dirty, bedraggled, the last hopeless heirs of the race, or trot in panic on their donkeys along the track in front of the train. You follow the "river with three names," the Urubamba, that storms over its boulders for tens of miles. You see the rope bridges spanning it; and then, when the gorge divides and you are at the bottom of the mountain hole, a furry cone of rock shoots upward for a couple thousand feet. On the wall opposite, out of sight from below, is the lost city, the condor's nest. There, terraced on the summit, with its altars open to the sky, its ruined windows turned for the rising and setting sun, its worshipers gone, is Machu Picchu.

—V. S. PRITCHETT, *At Home and Abroad*

January 20

ISTANBUL MASSAGE A LA TURK

*T*HEN IT'S MY TURN ON THE BROAD INLAID MARBLE massage slab called the *gobek tasi*. I'm rubbed, stretched and, at one point, mounted and pulled up by my arms before being taken off and soaped all over by a masseur who keeps saying "Good?" in a tone which brooks no disagreements. He dons a sinister black glove the size of a baseball mitt. (The brochure describes it as "a handknitted Oriental washing cloth," but it feels like a Brillo pad.) Never have I been so thoroughly scoured. The dirt and skin roll off me like deposits from a school rubber. How can I have been so filthy and not known about it?

—MICHAEL PALIN, *Pole to Pole*

ICEBERGS OFF OATES LAND, ANTARCTICA

SOME OF THE BERGS WERE OF MAGNIFICENT dimensions, one-third of a mile in length, and from one hundred and fifty to two hundred feet in height, with sides perfectly smooth, as though they had been chiseled. Others, again, exhibited lofty arches of many-coloured tints, leading into deep caverns, open to the swell of the sea, which rushing in, produced loud and distant thunderings. The flight of birds passing in and out of these caverns recalled the recollections of ruined abbeys, castles, and caves, while here and there a bold projecting bluff, crowned with pinnacles and turrets, resembled some Gothic keep…. If an immense city of ruined alabaster palaces can be imagined, of every variety and shape and tint, composed of huge piles of buildings grouped together, with long lanes or streets winding irregularly through them, some faint idea may be formed of the grandeur of the spectacle. The time and circumstances under which we were viewing them, threading our way through these vast bergs, we knew not to what end, left an impression upon me of these icy and desolate regions that can never be forgotten.

—CHARLES WILKES,
Narrative of the U.S. Exploring Expedition (1840)

January 22

ATOP THE MATTERHORN

*I*N THAT FIERCE MOMENT OF INTENSE LIVING WE FELT our blood surge within us. The terrors and struggles of the climb were forgotten. The abyss beneath us, the bewildering panorama about us, cast a spell that awed me to silence. I began to believe it awed Irvine too, for I saw him clasp his hands and look out over the six-thousand-foot chasm with an expression that assured me he was in tune with the Infinite.

"Oh, Dick," he whispered in such unusually solemn tones that I awaited some great inspired utterance about the sublimity of nature and the glory of God.

Breathlessly, tremblingly, I listened.

"*At last*," he continued in a faraway voice, "after talking about it and dreaming about it all these years, at last, I can *actually* SPIT A MILE!"

—RICHARD HALLIBURTON, *The Royal Road to Romance*

THE MANY FORMS OF TRAVEL

*J*OURNEYS, LIKE ARTISTS, ARE BORN AND NOT MADE. A thousand differing circumstances contribute to them, few of them willed or determined by the will—whatever we may think. They flower spontaneously out of the demands of our natures— and the best of them lead us not only outwards in space, but inwards as well. Travel can be one of the most rewarding forms of introspection.

—LAURENCE DURRELL, *Bitter Lemons*

January 24

A VISION OF THE MASAI

I'LL NEVER FORGET THE FIRST TIME I SAW A MASAI tribesman striding across the rolling grasslands of northern Tanzania. I was barreling along in a Land Rover with a photographer and a biologist—and there he was in the distance. Built like a willow, he moved over the landscape with long graceful strides. He wore sandals, a throw of red cloth, and a dagger slipped through the belt that held his dress in place. He carried only a spear and a gourd filled with milk or water. It was a humbling experience to watch him disappear over a slope of land, knowing he had miles to go before reaching his mud hut with its sparsely furnished interior.

—BUNNY MCBRIDE, "TRAVELING LIGHT"

TO RUSSIA, WITH LOVE

*I*NEVER IMAGINED I WOULD END UP IN RUSSIA, AND I certainly never expected to love it as I did. Growing up American, the only words I had to associate with Russia seemed to follow along a common course—words like red, threat, nuclear, cold war, and, of course, Communism. These words rang clear in my ears as I prepared for my trip. Russia is an enigma to so many of us in the U.S. and I yearned to see it for myself. I wanted to form my own opinion, free from any slanted political views my country had to offer.

The time I spent in Russia transformed the way I view other people, other countries, and myself. It challenged notions that were so ingrained that their source was virtually unrecognizable. I experienced the heartbeat of Russia, not the front page. I saw a beautifully lush country with rich history and fascinating people. Extensive parks of gold, brown, green, and amber replaced what I had thought would be endless rows of uniform concrete buildings. Vitality reigned where I was certain there would be despair and poverty. St. Petersburg overflowed with Dostoyevsky, ornamented old churches, and cobblestone roads. Life carries on in Russia, with a distinctive air of force and determination; my time there left me with a bit of that feeling tucked safely under my skin.

—CHRISTINE NIELSEN, "JUST MY IMAGINATION"

INVETERATE TRAVELER

*W*HAT ARE THE TELLTALE SIGNS OF THE inveterate traveler? She loves the act of traveling: the motion, the confusion of tickets and luggage, strangeness waiting like tickets to be opened.

What is home if the road that draws you away from it is more familiar, more comforting? Home is what you find when you get there. Home is any place on this planet. And no silver arch over the "Mighty Miss" to pin you there. They got some of us everywhere, Grandma said. In Ecuador, in 1977, on the seventh day of the seventh month, I stood at the equator: latitude 0'00. In Istanbul, I stood with one foot in Asia and the other in Europe.

The only sunrise I ever want to see is over the wingtip of a 747 at 35,000 feet. Otherwise, don't wake me before noon.

—COLLEEN J. McELROY, *A Long Way from St. Louie*

THE PERFECT PLACE

*W*E ALL HOLD A PLACE WITHIN OUR HEARTS—A perfect place—which is in the shape of an island. It provides refuge and strength; we can always retreat to its perfection. My mistake was to go there. Dreams should be nurtured and elaborated upon; they should never be visited. By going to Pitcairn, I had vanquished the perfect place within myself.

—DEA BIRKETT, *Serpent in Paradise*

January 28

SUNRISE

A T DAWN IN EAST AFRICA THE SKY BLEEDS RAW swatches of color, a violent beginning for someone used to gentler North American skies. In Vermont dawn is soft and light, a pale, porcelain-colored commencement that slowly builds into stronger hues and clarity. In Africa, the sun rises with passion, like a reckless, dangerous lover. It ignites the world in reds and golds and vaporizes cool mists collected overnight. Within minutes, the passion burns itself out and the long, hazy, colorless African day truly begins.

—DAVID EWING DUNCAN, *From Cape to Cairo*

January 29

SURVIVAL IN ANTARCTICA

*M*ANY OF THEM, IT SEEMED, FINALLY GRASPED FOR the first time just how desperate things really were. More correctly, they became aware of their own inadequacy, of how utterly powerless they were. Until the march from Ocean Camp they had nurtured in the backs of their minds the attitude Shackleton strove so unceasingly to imbue them with a basic faith in themselves—that they could, if need be, pit their strength and their determination against any obstacle—and somehow overcome it.

—ALFRED LANSING, *Endurance*

January 30

ROUNDABOUT IN INDIA

*I*N CHITTAURGARH (CITY OF VALOUR, SAID MY MAP) the man at the guest house knocked on my door and said, "Sir. Good evening but your country of origin is what please?"

"You've already written it down five times on five different bits of paper," I said.

"What is the fine name of your father?"

"You've written that five times as well."

"In the morning," he said, "you are wishing for a breakfast mealing?"

"Yes, that would be very nice. You have porridge?"

"Porridge—yes."

"Okay. One bowl porridge in the morning please."

"Porridge? No, no porridge."

"But you just said porridge—yes."

"No. Omelette, *chapatti*."

"Do you have yogurt—*dahi*?"

"*Dahi*. Yes."

"Okay, I'll have *dahi* then."

"Just *dahi*?"

"Yes, just *dahi*."

In the morning I was presented with a bowl of porridge.

—JOSIE DEW, *The Wind in My Wheels*

CUBA

*W*HEN FIRST IN THE DIM LIGHT OF EARLY MORNING I saw the shores of Cuba rise and define themselves from dark-blue horizons, I felt as if I sailed with Captain Silver and first gazed on Treasure Island. Here was a place where real things were going on. Here was a scene of vital action. Here was a place where anything might happen. Here was a place where something would certainly happen. Here I might leave my bones.

—SIR WINSTON CHURCHILL, *My Early Life*

THE LURE OF TRAVEL

*I*HAD LEFT AMERICA EXPECTING TO SPEND A MONTH, maybe two months, touring European castles, museums, and *bierfests*. Instead, the stories told by other travelers lured me first to Morocco, then toward the Middle East, across Turkey and Iran, and, during my seventh month, into Afghanistan. I recall my younger self as a dazed longhair gazing slack-jawed day after day at monuments, ruins, beguiling countrysides, and strange new cultures. From the bazaars of Marrakesh to the mosques of Istanbul and into the Hindu Kush, I could feel history and geography transforming me, and I fell stupidly in love with travel. I met other globe-roamers, and with them shared meals, beaches, and bus seats, and climbed peaks to celebrate sunsets. At night we huddled in cafes or around campfires, swapping tales and swearing that travel was the best thing that had ever happened to us, the best thing that could ever happen to anyone.

—BRAD NEWSHAM, *Take Me With You*

THE COURAGE TO EXPLORE

*T*HE FOREST IS EVERYWHERE. IT IS IN EVERY MAN, just as in every man is his own prison. Once you have escaped your prison, and gone through the forest and ocean of yourself, you do not need a retreat. You do not need a church or a monastery.

The world is open before you. All you need to do—and want to do—is walk through it.

—KENNETH WHITE, *Letters from Gourgounel*

February 3

SNAPSHOT

ONE MORNING WE AWOKE IN VENCE, A TOWN ABOVE Nice where the Matisse chapel is, in a room with long lace curtains covering the windows. The room glowed pink and our bed looked out into a magnolia tree long past bloom. Breakfast

was served on the terrace—café au lait, croissants, and marmalade. We planned to drive up into the mountains which eventually turned into the French Alps. The road wound around blind corners, dropped off into steep canyons. I clutched at the handle above my head, but was determined to kill

my ever-present fear. Finally we came to a wide valley and in the distance a stone village carved itself into the mountainside. I asked Bob to pull over and take my picture so I could remember what I look like when I wasn't afraid. Whenever I look at that picture now, I admire the woman in it and wonder who she is.

—MARGO HACKET, "FEARLESS IN FRANCE"

MEETING THE LOCALS

$\mathcal{M}$Y OWN LIFE HAS COMPELLED ME TO TRAVEL much and the process has convinced me that one never really knows another country unless one knows it through the life of the individuals who compose it. The characters revealed to us in newspapers and books or smeared on to the crowded international canvas tend to be more and more oversimplified and overdrawn until the responses of the individual suddenly acquire the dimensions of caricature. Even more than these cartoon inaccuracies, what alarmed me on my travels was the factors of impersonalization and dehumanization in the pictures countries painted for themselves of other nations, and years ago I began to cast around for correctives. I found the only effective one was holding on firmly in my imagination to such personal relationships as I had been able to form in foreign countries. I discovered that if I had but one clear portrait of an individual to which I could refer the collective abstractions that confronted me, their exaggeration and inaccuracy were speedily exposed. Finally this scaling down of monstrous oversimplifications to their fallible, questing, and constituent human proportions came to appear to me as one of the most urgent tasks of our day.

—LAURENS VAN DER POST, *A Portrait of All the Russias*

February 5

KNOW A PLACE WELL

BETTER FAR OFF TO LEAVE HALF THE RUINS AND nine-tenths of the churches unseen and to see well the rest; to see them not once, but again and again; to watch them, to learn them, to live with them, to love them, till they have become a part of life and life's recollections.

—AUGUSTUS HARE (1792-1834)

PACK LIGHTLY

$\mathscr{A}$T INVERNESS, THEREFORE, WE PROCURED THREE horses for ourselves and a servant, and one more for our baggage, which was no very heavy load. We found in the course of our journey the convenience of having disencumbered ourselves, by laying aside whatever we could spare, for it is not to be imagined without experience, how in climbing crags, and treading bogs, and winding through narrow and obstructed passages, a little bulk will hinder, and a little weight will burden; or how often a man that  has pleased himself at home with his own resolution, will, in the hour of darkness and fatigue, be content to leave behind him every thing but himself.

—SAMUEL JOHNSON,
A Journey to the Western Islands of Scotland (1775)

BREAK FREE

I FOUND I LIKED TO TRAVEL, BECAUSE IT GOT ME OUT OF my routines and my familiar patterns. The more traveling I did, the more organized I became. I kept adding things I liked to have with me on trips. Naturally I took books to read. Then I'd take my Walkman and the tapes I liked to listen to. Pretty soon I'd also take notebooks and colored pens for drawing. Then a portable computer for writing. Then magazines for the airplane trip. And a sweater in case it got cold on the airplane. And hand cream for dry skin.

Before long, traveling became a lot less fun, because now I was staggering onto airplanes, loaded down with all this stuff that I felt I had to take with me. I had made a new routine instead of escaping the old one. I wasn't getting away from the office any more: I was just carrying most of the contents of my desk on my shoulders.

So one day I decided I would get on the plane and carry nothing at all. Nothing to entertain me, nothing to save me from boredom…. What was I going to do?

It turned out I had a fine time. I read the magazines that were on the plane. I talked to people. I stared out the window. I thought about things.

It turned out I didn't need any of that stuff I thought I needed. In fact, I felt a lot more alive without it.

—MICHAEL CRICHTON, *Travels*

NOTRE DAME

*I*N ALL DIRECTIONS I SAW MAGNIFICENT AISLES, AND altars with burning incense. Magnificent pictures representing all revered worth, from the "Son of Man" to saints of France. Golden knobs with inscriptions thereon, adorned the footsteps of every visitor thereof, denoting the downwardness of kings who had once ruled nations. Whilst standing awestruck with departed worth, I gazed downward with a submissive heart, when lo! I stood upon the coffin of a King! I quickly changed my position, but stepped upon a Queen. The valet was relating to me the many different opinions the people had about stepping on noted personages, and how unnecessary it was to take notice of such things as they were dead, when I got disgusted at his ignorance and stepped from a Queen to a Princess.

—DAVID F. DORR,
A Colored Man Round the World (1858)

HOME IS NOT HOME UNTIL YOU RETURN

Y OUR TRAVEL LIFE HAS THE ESSENCE OF A DREAM. It is something outside the normal, yet you are in it. It is peopled with characters you have never seen before and in all probability will never see again. It brings occasional homesickness, and loneliness, and pangs of longing…. But you are like the Vikings or the master mariners of the Elizabethan age, who have gone into a world of adventure, and home is not home until you return.

—AGATHA CHRISTIE (1890–1976)

A SALUTE TO THE ANDES

*Y*EARS BEFORE, ON MY FIRST VISIT TO THE ANDES, I'D learned that mountains were not metaphors for wilderness, but entities in themselves. Walking above Cuzco, I'd met an old man who spoke some Spanish. I'd point to a dazzling snow-capped mountain and asked its name.

"Apu Auzangate," he said.

"And that one?" I pointed to another.

"Apu Salkantay."

"*Apu* means mountain?"

He squinted at Salkantay, and held up his hand in salute.

"It means the god in that place: Salkantay."

At the head of the valley was the craggy peak whose shoulder formed one half of the pass we aimed to cross: Apu Taulliraju. I saluted like the old man had and hoped for the best.

—JANINE POMMY VEGA, *Tracking the Serpent*

RISE WITH A NEW VIEW

I'VE DONE IT SEVERAL TIMES BEFORE IN AFRICA—GONE to bed in a dark hotel room fighting depression, if not downright hysteria, and then wakened to sunlight and beauty and thoughts of what a fool I had been. Within the first ten minutes of strolling down Main Street toward the waterfront, I was in love with Zanzibar.

—MARGARET G. RYAN, *African Hayride*

A SOLITARY LANDSCAPE

*P*EOPLE WHO KNOW NOTHING ABOUT THESE THINGS will tell you that there is no addition of pleasure in having a landscape to yourself. But this is not true. It is a pleasure exclusive, unreasoning, and real: it has some of the quality and some of the intensity of love: it is a secret shared: a communion which an intruder desecrates: and to go to the lonely and majestic places of the world for poor motives, to turn them to cheap advertisement or flashy journalism, jars like a spiritual form of prostitution on your true lover of the hills. The solitary rapture must be disinterested. And often it is stumbled upon unthinkingly by men whose business takes them along remoter ways: who suddenly find enchantment on their path and carry it afterwards through their lives with a secret sense of exile.

—FREYA STARK, *The Valleys of the Assassins*

A PLACE OF RETREAT

*B*UT BY FAR THE MOST LOVELY THING I SAW IN Isfahan, one of those things whose loveliness endures as a melody in the mind, was the Madrasseh, meaning school; but if a school at all, then a school for pensiveness, for contemplation, for spiritual withdrawal; a school in which to learn to be alone. A cloister, not in the architectural sense of the word, but in the psychological; a place of retreat and harmony, open to all, but where each one might go to arrive or to depart, unnoticed, unquestioned, in that independence which few communities understand or are willing to accord. One is allowed to be lonely there; but in more civilized communities no one is allowed to be lonely; the refinement of loneliness is not understood.

—VITA SACKVILLE-WEST, *Passenger to Tehran* (1926)

LOVE OF PLACE

*I*t isn't necessarily the great and famous beauty spots we fall in love with. As with people, so with places: love is unforeseen, and we can all find ourselves affectionately attached to the minor and the less obvious. I do not have an art historian's response to places. I can discern and admire a late-Renaissance gate, a medieval street, a Romanesque church, or an Etruscan wall, but my first thoughts are for the warmth of the stone or for the clouds, when they look like a fifteenth-century painting with a chariot or a saint zooming up into them. I notice the light and shade on buildings grouped on a hilltop, the rich skin colors and the shapes of the people around me. I love to watch people, to sit in a trattoria listening in to their talk, imagining the rest.

—MURIEL SPARK, "SIDE ROADS OF TUSCANY"

REALIZE YOUR TRAVEL DREAMS

*T*RAVEL MAKES UP FOR ITS DISCOMFORTS BY supplying passengers with megadoses of a supplementary vitamin, the need for which in human nutrition may not yet have been established but whose presence in a trip has a bracing effect upon an individual. This is the exhilarating sense of adventure which, when all is said and done, is what travel is all about. Travel stripped of adventure is almost inevitably an exercise imbedded in monotony; without it the traveler moves through strange lands untouched and touching nothing. I have been pulled out of quicksand in an Amazon jungle, I have spent the best part of a winter's day locked up in Elsinore Castle, and I once swam in the Coral Sea in an area that I was told—later—was the greatest breeding place in the world for sharks, but these are not necessarily the adventures that travelers need experience. Perhaps what I want to say is that one should use travel as a means of living out fantasies, of making the bright dream materialize.

—CASKIE STINNETT, *Grand and Private Pleasures*

THE PRAYER WHEEL

*W*E STOPPED TO VISIT A BUDDHIST TEMPLE. NEMA, our guide, took hold of the wheel's twisted rope and began walking the worn path. At the completion of one rotation the wheel tripped a bell. After three rotations Nema encouraged me to do the same while making an unselfish wish.

Taking hold of the handle I began walking but found myself unable to focus on a wish, unselfish or otherwise. I seemed to have spent a lifetime dreaming of travel and adventure, but finally on such a journey, I found myself wondering why I was here and what I was looking for. *Ding*, the bell signaled my first rotation.

I had known I was coming to Nepal for nearly a year and had read in preparation. I think it had been easier to focus on cultural differences rather than similarities. *Ding*, the bell signaled my second rotation.

My readings, instead of helping to immerse me into the culture, had made me look at my trek from a factual, detached point of view. This approach reflected what I had done to so much of my life. The wheel groaned with its fullness of unselfish wishes, and impulsively I wished for those wishes to be fulfilled. *Ding*, the bell signaled my third rotation.

I found myself deeply moved and deeply changed. Entering the room as a traveler I left it a pilgrim.

—KIRK GRACE, "THE PRAYER WHEEL," *Travelers' Tales Nepal*

FINDING YOUR PLACE IN THE WORLD

*U*P IN THE HIGH AIR, YOU BREATHED EASILY, drawing in a vital assurance and lightness of heart. In the highlands you woke up in the morning and thought: Here I am, where I ought to be.

—ISAK DINESEN, *Out of Africa*

A CHANCE DESTINATION

"WHERE IS ALCOY?" I ASKED.

"Hmm," he took a moment to think over the question, looking carefully at the precipitous scenery outside the window. "Next stop, I think."

"Next stop?" I echoed.

"Yes, next stop."

"How soon is that do you think?" Before he could respond, the conductor entered our car calling, "Xativa, Alcoy, Ontivent, all out for Zativa, Albaida, Cocentaina, and Alcoy."

I admit there was a moment of hesitation. Granada was in my mind, in my plans, and was printed on my ticket. But just ahead Alcoy was beckoning, a Moorish maiden behind a veil, a prize hidden in a box of Cracker Jack, an unsolicited invitation to a game of chance. Alcoy was on the front page before me. I looked again at the photo held between Ernesto's hands. I didn't have to ask.

"Go," he said simply, as much with his oversized eyes as his soft voice. "I have always wanted to see this myself. You will like it."

As the train slowed, my heart quickened. I stood up, shouldered my pack, and thanked Ernesto, shaking his hand. As I turned to go he said, "Here, take these." He gave me the newspapers and a final lingering glance. I stepped off the car, into the unexpected.

—JOEL SIMON, "YESTERDAY'S PAPER," *Travelers' Tales Spain*

February 19

TEA AND CARPETS

*W*HEN THE ENGLISH-SPEAKING MOHAMID cha-cha'd into the room with all the dramatics of an overacted stage play and poured me a second glass of mint tea, I was ready to tell him not to launch into any sales pitches. I never got the chance. Forty-five minutes may have passed, but I can't be sure, of Mohamid waving his body back and forth, his eyes never averting from mine. I sat transfixed, hypnotized, moving in time to his rhythm. Pots of mint tea kept coming from other rooms while Mohamid entranced me with carpet yarns.

At some point, I recall babbling, "Carpets, carpets, yes, I want carpets…carpets…."

—LAURIE GOUGH, *Kite Strings of the Southern Cross*

THE KINDNESS OF STRANGERS

I WAS TRAVELING AROUND EUROPE AT MY LEISURE. WHEN I arrived in Amsterdam without reservations, I was distressed to find that the entire city was overtaken by Germans on holiday. I carried my bulky backpack up and down the canals, searching for a vacancy. Exhausted, I parked myself in a phone booth and went through my guidebook calling every accommodation listed. I finally found an expensive B&B that had miraculously had a cancellation minutes before I called. "I'll take it."

That night I went to an underground club I had read about online, and was surprised when a couple of local Dutch women started talking to me. For hours we discussed my travel and their life in Holland. Without even mentioning my predicament, one of the women, Inge, invited me to stay with her in Leiden. "You must see the Holland that exists outside of Amsterdam."

She didn't have to extend such an offer, and I couldn't believe I was actually taking her up on it. Two days later I found myself on a train to the university town, walking along a gorgeous canal, and stopping to knock on a big black door. Inge opened it and we ascended the tiny, steep Dutch stairs. During the time we spent together, she showed me Leiden, Den Haag, Arnhem, Delft, Gouda, and Groningen, introducing me to *poofertjies,* white bicycles, and her friends and family.

The greatest gift of travel is the connection you make with strangers—and the transition that occurs from foreigner to friend.

—LISA BACH, "A TOUR OF HOLLAND"

THE AESTHETIC OF ITALY

*A*S WITH THE STUDY OF ITALIAN PICTURES, SO IT IS
with Italy itself. The country is divided, not
in *partes tres*, but in two: a foreground and a
background. The foreground is the property
of the guide-book and of its product, the
mechanical sight-seer; the background, that
of the dawdler, the dreamer, and the serious
student of Italy. This distinction does
not imply any depreciation of the
foreground. It must be known
thoroughly before the middle
distance can be enjoyed: there is
no short cut to an intimacy with Italy.

—EDITH WHARTON, *Italian Backgrounds* (1905)

DEEP EXPLORATION

I CLAMBERED UP THE SLICK ROCK, FOLLOWING A tenuous crack system. Traveling across slick rock is something between climbing, scrambling, and delicate walking: you tiptoe up, pressing your fingertips against the stone for balance, until the gradient becomes too steep and you have to pull yourself up, using nubbins and hollows for handholds. The rock rolls away in every direction, a steep, smooth sea of reds, grays, bone-whites. It is a graceful realm that almost forces you to move with grace.

As I moved up through the slick rock, my shadow stretched out long and lithe in the slanting sun; the crack widened to a crevice. An elegant black ribbon of old water raveled down the gilded stone. I emerged into a kind of miniature amphitheater in the canyon wall; in its center was a *tinaja*, a natural tank of old water ten or twelve feet deep, cold and clear as a diamond. No one had ever been in that place before; I was the first; I could feel it in my bones.

—ROB SCHULTHEIS, *The Hidden West*

TASMANIA

*F*ROM THE AIR, TASMANIA IS ALIEN, INTRACTABLE. That day on the plane I felt amazed and ashamed that I'd lived on the edge of this wild immensity and had known nothing about it. But if I had known, how could I have coped with the knowledge? That lost world won't ever be conquered; the rest of Tasmania is habitable only under duress, in narrow valleys between the mountains. Living there, you resolve not to notice, or else you'd be demoralized forever. My tendency too, after that aerial survey, was to burrow. Up above, it may look desolate. Down below, crushed and compressed under ground, there is a weird, subliminal beauty—a surreal Tasmania guarded in darkness.

—PETER CONRAD, *Behind the Mountain*

IMPRESSIONS OF PARADISE

*T*HIS ADVENTURE IN PARADISE HAD STARTED LONG ago with a banana. I was a schoolboy in New Zealand, doing the weekend errands, when the greengrocer piled potatoes on the scales until the pointer quivered at five pounds. As he tumbled them into my basket he said he had a love letter for me. From the South Seas, he added, licking the stub of a pencil hanging from his neck on a string and jotting the cost of the spuds on a paper bag.

That a letter of any kind should be addressed to me care of the fruit and vegetable man at the end of our road was mystifying. That it should be a love letter, and from the South Seas, was lunatic. Then Jan, a grave Dutchman not usually given to practical jokes, handed me a banana and urged me to read it.

The sneer died in my throat as I realized the banana did indeed bear a message. In rough cuts of a broad thumbnail, which would have been invisible when the banana was hard and green and packed in its crate but now were clearly legible in brown on mottled yellow, the banana proclaimed:

DEAR JOHN, I LOVE YOU. SEXY DOROTHY.

—JOHN DYSON, *The South Seas Dream*

February 25

THE BEAUTY OF LAHAINA

I HAVE BEEN SPENDING THE DAY AT LAHAINA ON MAUI, on my way from Kawaihae to Honolulu. Lahaina is thoroughly beautiful and tropical looking, with its white latticed houses peeping out from under coco palms, breadfruit, candlenut, tamarinds, mangoes, bananas, and oranges, with the brilliant green of a narrow strip of sugar-cane for a background, and above, the flushed mountains of Eeka, riven here and there by cool green chasms, rise to a height of 6,000 feet. Beautiful Lahaina! It is an oasis in a dazzling desert, straggling for nearly two miles along the shore, but compressed into a width of half a mile....

The beach is formed of pure white broken coral; the sea is blue with the calm, pure blue of turquoise, but crystalline in its purity, and breaks forever over the environing coral reef with a low deep music. Blue water stretched to the far horizon, the sky was blazing blue, the leafage was almost dazzling to the eye, the mountainous island of Molokai floated like a great blue morning glory on the yet bluer sea; a sweet, soft breeze rustled through the palms, lazy ripples plashed lightly on the sand; humanity basked, flower-clad, in sunny indolence; everything was redundant, fervid, beautiful.

—ISABELLA BIRD, *Six Months in the Sandwich Islands* (1873)

THE RHYTHM OF THE BRAZILIAN NIGHT

*D*ENSE RHYTHMS CROSS AND DANCE WITH EACH other, each grabbing hold of the crowd in a different way. By now, the sound is deafening and conversations are out of the question. Everyone is dancing, the sweat flows, and the balmy night air carries more than a hint of eroticism with all the men and women wearing so little and drinking so much. The festive atmosphere is euphoric, as worries and cares are sent flying. There's no doubt in anyone's mind: samba is what it's all about.

—CHRIS MCGOWAN AND RICARDO PESSANHA,
The Brazilian Sound

NEW ORLEANS

*I*N NEW ORLEANS LIFE IS A PEDESTRIAN. PEOPLE navigate their streets like fish: the streets are our medium, a fluid and changing spectacle that is also the stuff we breathe in and out. It's a city for watching and being watched, a voyeur-voyee paradise that reaches an apogee at Carnival, when everything that can be shown is made manifest, everything that was hidden is displayed, and one's senses are ambushed. At Mardi Gras the city becomes impassable to cars. A swelling humanity moves in and out of itself, full of mysterious and alive intimacy that the drivers of America never experience. New Orleans at Carnival is seditious, un-American, sabotage incarnate—what General Motors sees in nightmares! The huge motorized floats at the head of Mardi Gras parades are grotesque parodies of cars. They insult cars. They move at a pace slower than that of most people. Masked demons perched on top of them shower the intoxicated mob with doubloons, jewels, cigars, panties, and coconuts. People lean on parked cars, sleep on top of them, use them for planters and ashtrays.

—ANDREI CODRESCU, *Road Scholar*

REMEMBER

*T*HE AMERICAN WHO VISITS EUROPE FOR THE FIRST time is apt to be in a hurry, and to endeavor to see too much.... Instances have occurred of tourists who could not tell whether St. Paul's Cathedral was in London or Rome, and who had a vague impression that the tomb of Napoleon was beneath the Arc de Triomphe. They told of the wonderful wood-carving to be seen at Venice, and thought that Michaelangelo, John Titian, and Sir Christopher Wren were among the most famous painters Switzerland had ever produced....

Moral—Don't be in a hurry.

—THOMAS W. KNOX, *How to Travel* (1881)

March 1

THE ESSENCE OF MY SELF

*S*OME PEOPLE, I SUPPOSE, USE THE ANONYMITY OF travel to pretend they are something they are not. They even tell tales.

But stripped of the trappings of home, I think we actually become the essence of ourselves. With nothing familiar behind which to hide, we are left completely to the resources that live only within us. The brave are at their bravest, the fearful confront their timidity.

We are different people when we travel because there is no other time when we are so utterly ourselves. It is both terrifying and refreshing and always, always enlightening.

—SOPHIA DEMBLING, "YEARNING FOR FARAWAY PLACES"

SITTING ON THE DOCK OF BOMBAY

*T*HEN ONE MORNING THE DESERT VASTNESS OF THE dock was quickened with activity, and it was as if the silent film had become a silent epic. Long rows of two-toned taxicabs were drawn up outside the terminal building; scattered all over the dock area, as though awaiting a director's call to action, were black little clusters of horsecabs; and steadily, through the dock gates, far to the right, more taxis and cabs came rolling in. The horses galloped, the drivers' ship hands worked. It was a brief exaltation. Soon enough for each cab came repose at the edge of a cab-cluster. The cause of the excitement was presently seen: a large white liner, possibly carrying tourists, possibly carrying ten-pound immigrants to Australia. Slowly, silently, she idled in. And more taxis came pelting through the gates, and more cabs, racing in feverishly to an anti-climax of nosebags and grass.

The liner docked early in the morning. It was not until noon that the first passengers came out of the terminal building into the wasteland of the dock area. This was like the director's call…. But this was not to be. Just when the passengers had been penned by cabs and taxis, and gestures of remonstrance had given way to stillness, so that it seemed escape was impossible and capture certain, two shiny motorcoaches came through the dock gates…and where before there had been tourists in gay cottons, there was now only asphalt.

—V. S. NAIPAUL, *An Area of Darkness*

March 3

LA PAZ, BOLIVIA

*T*O BE ENCLOSED BETWEEN TWO lofty ranges and two deserts, to live at the bottom of a hole and yet be nearly as high above sea level as the top of the Rocky Mountains or the Jungfrau, are strange conditions for a dwelling place. Nevertheless, it was a place in which one might do much meditation.

—JAMES BRYCE, *South America* (1912)

THE LEGACY OF TRAVEL

*W*HEN I WAS A BOY IN SCHOOL MY FAVORITE subject was geography, and my prize possession my geography book. This book was filled with pictures of the world's most wonderful cities and mountains and temples, and had big maps to show where they were. I loved that book because it carried me away to all the strange and romantic lands. I read about the Egyptian Pyramids, and India's marble towers, about the great cathedrals of France, and the ruins of ancient Babylon. The stories of such things always set me to dreaming, to yearning for the actual sight and touch of these world wonders.

Sometimes I pretended I had a magic carpet, and without bothering about tickets and money and farewells, I'd skyrocket away to New York or to Rome, to the Grand Canyon or to China, across deserts and oceans and mountains...then suddenly come back home when the school bell rang for recess.

I often said to myself: "I wish my father, or somebody, would take me to all these wonderful places. What good are they if you can't see them? If I ever grow up and have a son, we are going traveling together. I'll show him Gibraltar and Jerusalem, the Andes and the Alps, because I'll want my boy not only to study geography—I'd like for him to live it, too."

—RICHARD HALLIBURTON, *The Complete Book of Marvels*

NORTHERN LIGHTS

*T*HE FIRST NIGHT I RELUCTANTLY PULLED ON MY coat, boots, fleece hat, neck gaiter, and gloves, then scrambled and slid down the haphazard path to the three-sided outhouse. Sitting there, pants down, bottom pasted against the frosty wood, I felt crabby and ridiculous, vulnerable and exposed, and cold, incurably cold. Then starting back up the path, I saw the sky spread out over the lake in white ribbons and columns of light, then reappear in green. The Northern Lights. The colors flickered and pulsed against the blacker darkness in an incredible display. All I could do was stand and marvel, and send my tiny speck of energy, my consciousness, out to greet the sky.

—MARY HUSSMAN, "NORTH"

KNOW THE WORLD

A SPIRITUAL NECESSITY...TRAVEL MUST RANK with the more serious forms of endeavor. Admittedly there are other ways of making the world's acquaintance. But the traveler is a slave to his senses; his grasp of a fact can only be complete when reinforced by sensory evidence; he can know the world, in fact, only when he sees, hears, and smells it.

—ROBERT BYRON, *The Road to Oxiana*

Pyramids

> The mighty pyramids of stone
> That wedge-like cleave the desert airs,
> When nearer seen and better known,
> Are but gigantic flights of stairs.

—H. W. Longfellow,
The Ladder of St. Augustine (1850)

SOUTH ATLANTIC OCEAN

*W*HILE SAILING A LITTLE SOUTH OF THE PLATA ON one very dark night, the sea presented a wonderful and most beautiful spectacle. There was a fresh breeze, and every part of the surface, which during the day is seen as foam, now glowed with a pale light. The vessel drove before her bows two billows of liquid phosphorous, and in her wake she was followed by a milky train. As far as the eye reached, the crest of every wave was bright and the sky above the horizon, from the reflected glare of these livid flames, was not so utterly obscure as over the vault of the heavens.

—CHARLES DARWIN, *Journal During the Voyage of H.M.S. Beagle* (1832–36)

THE SPIRIT OF INDIA

*S*O BEAUTIFUL HAVE BEEN THE DAYS OF THIS YEAR. I have seen a love that would be one with the humblest and most ignorant, seeing the world for a moment through his eyes. I have laughed at the colossal caprice of genius; I have warmed myself by heroic fires and have been present at the awakening of a holy child… My companions and I played with God and knew it… The scales fell from our eyes and we saw that all indeed are one and we are condemned no more. We worship neither pain nor pleasure. We seek through either to come to that which transcends them both… Only in India is the religious life perfectly conscious and fully developed.

—SISTER NIVEDITA (1867–1905)

EX-PATRIOTISM

*S*AINT-GERMAIN WAS ALWAYS THE LITERARY QUARTER and, until the American influx of the early 1920s, quiet and bourgeois. Each year, the increasing number of us there assumed a sort of outpost quality. We were the Americans who, for one reason or another, chose to dwell in Paris—for writing, for work, for career, for the amenities of French living, which was cheaper and more agreeable than life in the United States. My satisfaction in living there was double: I felt I was living both at home and abroad—living surrounded with the human familiarity of American friends and acquaintances, and the constant, shifting stimulation that came from the native French.

—JANET FLANNER, *Paris Was Yesterday*

FEAR

*W*HAT GIVES VALUE TO TRAVEL IS FEAR. IT IS THE fact that, at a certain moment, when we are so far from our own country we are seized by a vague fear, and an instinctive desire to go back to the protection of old habits. This is the most obvious benefit of travel. At that moment we are feverish but also porous, so that the slightest touch makes us quiver to the depths of our being. We come across a cascade of light, and there is eternity. This is why we should not say that we travel for pleasure.

—ALBERT CAMUS (1913–1960)

TIMELESS BUDDHA

*A*FTER LUNCH WE STARTED OUT IN RICKSHAWS AND spent the afternoon dawdling in and out of beautiful temples. I can't tell you how wonderful they are and the extraordinary sense of peace about them all. The plum trees lift white branches over the shrines and camellias drop their scarlet flowers upon all the paths. This place was once a great capital; it was washed away by a tidal wave in the fifteenth century, but there remains one masterpiece of the old time, a colossal Bronze Buddha. His temple was carried out to sea; and he sits all alone in a beautiful garden with bronze lotus plants in front of him and he is the most solemn and impressive thing in Japan.

—GERTRUDE BELL, LETTER (1898)

March 13

TRAVEL IS *LOVELY*

W HEN I THINK BACK OVER MY TRAVELS, I FEEL profoundly lucky. Images from various places keep coming into my mind. The voice I most often hear on the soundtrack belongs to Giustino, a displaced Italian chef who drank at The Fountain and carried on conversations in a bastard mix of languages. Every Sunday, he went to a street market to shop for the big meal he cooked for his wife, and he liked to show me what he'd bought. He'd yank the food from his shopping bag—vegetables, beefsteak, red wine—and display it on the bar. Then he'd step away to admire the arrangement. This was a version of the cosmos, how it ought to be. "Lovely," Giustino would say, kissing his fingertips. "*Lovely*!" I know of no better description of my own time on the road.

—BILL BARICH, *Traveling Light*

GETTING AWAY FROM IT ALL

*W*HENEVER PEOPLE TELL ME HOW PASSIONATELY they desire to Get Away From It All, I think I know what is in their mind's eye. They see themselves riding off into the sunset, or paddling a canoe down the silver wake of the moon, or very slowly (but ecstatically) stretching their arms on the edge of a huge precipice; they see themselves, in fact, in terms of the silent film. They imagine some vast solitude with a healthy climate, where no telephones ring and no maids give notice, where there are no income-tax returns and incidentally no insects: where the Simple Life is possible.

Such an Arden, though it may exist, would not, I fear, be as they like it. But where they make their gravest error is in supposing, as dramatists and film directors have license to suppose, that the process of Getting Away From It All has a climax, that there comes a sharp, sweet moment when the escaper consciously relishes the full flavor of escape. In my experience, no such moment exists. We do not, today, cut loose. We wriggle out of one complicated existence like a snake sloughing its skin, and by the time we have wriggled into the next it has become complicated too…. The old life overlaps what should have been the most exhilarating moments of the new; the first stage on the golden road to Samarkand has no enchantment for the man who is doubtful whether they packed his evening shoes.

—PETER FLEMING, *One's Company*

March 15

MEXICO

NOWHERE MORE THAN IN MEXICO DOES HUMAN life become isolated, external to its surroundings, and cut off tinily from the environment. Even as you come across the plain to a big city like Guadalajara, and see the twin towers of the cathedral peering around in loneliness like two lost birds side by side on a moor, lifting their white heads to look around in the wilderness, your heart gives a clutch, feeling the pathos, the isolated tininess of human effort. As for building a church with one tower only, it is unthinkable. There must be two towers, to keep each other company in this wilderness world.

—D. H. LAWRENCE, *Mornings in Mexico*

IRELAND

I FIND IRELAND HOLDS FASCINATION, a sense of magic and mystery, riddle and rhyme, darkness and blinding light; much of it readily apparent, but deeper shades shimmering beneath the surface, like layers of green that finally catch the sun. I've always wanted to stay and know more. Ireland is Gaelic and Celtic, Wolfe Tones and banshees...the light and dark of all of us.

—KAREN EBERHARDT, "DREAMING IN GREEN"

March 17

WOMEN'S TRAVEL

*T*HE MONOTONY OF OUR SAFARI WAS SHATTERED BY a frightening experience. We approached a village in the early morning hours. I was looking forward to stretching my legs. As we entered the village, a group of men gathered before us. They shouted, "*Pagal, Pagal!*" in threatening voices. One old man appeared with a rifle and made nasty gestures. Abdul did not utter a word. He prodded our animals to move quickly out of town. The men followed behind our caravan screaming insults until we were far from their town. Abdul explained to me that the villagers felt that apart from locals, only lunatics would come to such a remote place. A lone woman could only mean trouble. She must therefore be a witch. They wanted no part of us and our bad luck. Most likely I would never again have such an honor. I had been labeled mad and then banished as a witch.

—MARYBETH BOND, "THE END OF THE ROAD,"
A Woman's World

No Conscious Plan

*T*HE SPIRIT OF MAN IS NOMAD, HIS BLOOD BEDOUIN, and love is the Aboriginal tracker on the faded desert spoor of his lost self; and so I came to live my life not by conscious plan or prearranged design but as someone following the flight of a bird.

—LAURENS VAN DER POST,
A Walk with a White Bushman

March 19

TIMBUKTU

*W*E WERE DRIVING HARD FOR TIMBUKTU THROUGH the desert at night. It was midnight and I came up over a rise, and there in the distance were the bright lights of Timbuktu: twenty-seven of them. I counted. When I got in I did some very serious and intensive investigative reporting, and I can tell you that it is impossible to get a cold beer in Timbuktu on a Saturday night at 12:30. I could get a warm beer—but not a cold one. Timbuktu is essentially a dusty adobe town with courtyards. There is a mosque—a mud mosque—of great antiquity but of no great distinction. At one time in the twelfth century, Timbuktu was a center of Islamic learning and there were more than eighty Koranic schools there. They still have some of those old texts, and they are the coolest thing to see in Timbuktu. The other thing is the post office, because everybody goes to the post office and has their postcard stamped "Timbuktu."

—TIM CAHILL, "INTERVIEW"

NEW YORK HARBOR

I HAVE NEVER SEEN THE BAY OF Naples. I can therefore make no comparison, but my imagination is incapable of conceiving any thing of the kind more beautiful than the harbor of New York. Various and lovely are the objects which meet the eye on every side, but naming them would only be to give a list of words, without conveying the faintest idea of the scene. I doubt if ever the pencil of Turner could do it justice, bright and glorious as it rose upon us. We seemed to enter the harbor of New York upon waves of liquid gold, and as we darted past the green isles which rise from its bosom, like guardian sentinels of the fair  city, the setting sun stretched his horizontal beams farther and farther at each moment, as if to point out to us some new glory in the landscape.

—MRS. FRANCES TROLLOPE,
Domestic Manners of the Americans (1832)

THE CHERRY BLOSSOM FRONT IS MOVING IN

*E*VERY SPRING, A WAVE OF FLOWERS SWEEPS ACROSS Japan. It begins in Okinawa and rolls from island to island to mainland. It hits at Cape Sata and moves north, cresting as it goes, to the very tip of distant Hokkaido, where it scatters and falls into a northern sea.

They call it Sakura Zensen—the "Cherry Blossom Front"— and its advance is tracked with a seriousness usually reserved for armies on the march. Progress reports are given nightly on the news and elaborate maps are prepared to show the front lines, the back lines, and the percentage of blossoms in any one area. "In Shimabara today they reported thirty-seven percent full blossoms."

Nowhere on earth does spring arrive as dramatically as it does in Japan. When the cherry blossoms hit, they hit like a hurricane. Gnarled cherry trees, ignored for most of the year, burst into bloom like fountains turned suddenly on.

—WILL FERGUSON, *Hokkaido Highway Blues*

A DIP IN THE DEAD SEA

I BATHED IN THE DEAD SEA. THE GROUND COVERED by the water sloped so gradually that I was not only forced to "sneak in," but to walk through the water nearly a quarter of a mile, before I could get out of my depth. When at last I was able to attempt to dive, the salts held in solution made my eyes smart so sharply, that the pain I thus suffered, joined with the weakness occasioned by want of food, made me giddy and faint for some moments; but I soon grew bitter. I knew beforehand the impossibility of sinking in this buoyant water; but I was surprised to find that I could not swim at my accustomed pace: my legs and feet were lifted so high and dry out of the lake, that my stroke was baffled, and I found myself kicking against the thin air, instead of the dense fluid upon which I was swimming. The water is perfectly bright and clear; its taste detestable. After finishing my attempts at swimming and diving, I took some time in regaining the shore, and, before I began to dress, I found that the sun had already evaporated the water which clung to me, and that my skin was thickly encrusted with salts.

—A. W. KINGLAKE, *Eothen* (1844)

March 23

ON THE WAY TO CLASS

I WAS STUDYING SPANISH IN TAXCO, MEXICO, WHERE school was a ten-minute walk from my rented apartment. One day while walking to Spanish class, I counted twenty dogs of every size and variety. Some dogs barked at me, some simply laid there worshiping the Mexican morning sun. The sheer combination of breeds astounded me, some with legs too long for their short bodies, some blending five breeds into one trembling mass with a nose too long. I passed young girls with their arms around each other's shoulders, usually the younger one hugging the older—creating a tight bond, two strong girls against the world, ignoring everyone in their path. I passed children with clothes so dirty that they had become another color. Girls younger than myself, much younger, carried bundles so small that I had to look closely to confirm that yes, they were babies. Church bells rang incessantly and I realized I was late for class once again.

—KRISTA HOLMSTROM, "While in Taxco"

UNIVERSAL TRUTHS

*T*HE ROAD CARRIED US THROUGH VILLAGES AND farm fields as it climbed higher and higher towards the rim of the valley. The mustard fields glowed iridescent yellow against a background of emerald green rice paddies. Hugging and puffing, we were no doubt a curious sight to behold in the eyes of the average villager. Two women, unescorted, dressed in t-shirts and colorful local-style baggy pants (little did they know we had our specialized bike shorts on underneath!), eyes hidden behind dark glasses, a steep hill when everybody in their right mind walks, and slowly at that.

As we stopped for a breather at the top of a particularly steep pitch, a wizened, barefoot farmer of indeterminate age appeared from nowhere. He walked right up to us and assessed us from head to foot from behind thick glasses.

"Long suffering?" he asked us in most polite English. It wasn't really a question, it was more of a statement. Wendy and I immediately understood the metaphysical implications of his pronouncement.

"Yes, yes!" we heartily agreed, giddy from the intense physical exertion and the comic clarity of coming face-to-face with a universal truth.

—MAUREEN DECOURSEY, "MOUNTAIN BIKING WITH WENDY,"
Travelers' Tales Nepal

March 25

BOGOTA, COLOMBIA

BOGOTA IS A CITY OF CONVERSATION. AS YOU WALK along you have to keep skirting couples or small groups, all absorbed in excited talk. Some of them even stand out in the middle of the street, holding up the traffic. We suppose they are discussing politics. The cafes are crammed, too; and everybody has a newspaper, to quote from or simply wave in the air.

—CHRISTOPHER ISHERWOOD, *The Condor and the Cows*

CHANGE OF SEASONS

*I*T IS THE SMELLS OF A STRANGE CITY THAT GRADUALLY lure one into its inner mysteries, and in Moscow these were rich, strange, and various, especially in summer: a blend of low-grade petrol fumes, cheap calico, black *mahorka* tobacco, disinfectant, the warm yeasty odor of freshly-baked bread, and the slightly acrid smell of tar when the water-cart has passed. Then as the days lengthened and the dry breath of the surrounding plains invaded the city, the *topol,* or white poplar, shed its fluffy seeds upon the air, where they slowly sank to gather in great bleached drifts along the pavement edge, like a parody of snowfalls past or still to come.

—ERIK DE MAUNY, *Russian Prospect*

March 27

MANCHURIA, CHINA

*T*O MY MIND MANCHURIA IS INFINITELY MORE beautiful in its leafless state than in summer. When the kowliang is cut the hidden undulations and delicate lines are revealed. It is a country of exquisite outlines. When one sees the rare trees, with their frail fretwork of branches standing out in dark and intricate patterns against the rosy haze of the wintry sunset, suffused and softened with innumerable particles of brown dust, one realizes whence Chinese art drew its inspiration; one understands how the "cunning working in Pekin" pricked onto porcelain the colors and designs which make Oriental china beautiful and precious.

—MAURICE BARING, *What I Saw in Russia* (1913)

THE SCENT OF TRAVEL

I AM HOPING NOW TO KEEP WONDER AND CURIOSITY alive, in the age of armchair and video travel, by recalling the smell, the one thing that you can never write down, film, or bring back, that will always remind you of a place or a person. Because it can never be recorded except in the mind, smell is the most intimate and the most mnemonic of the senses, linked to appetite and, through that, sex.

The smell of Africa and the Caribbean is that of palm oil, used for cooking, a cloying, soapy odor to me. North America smells like the inside of an empty refrigerator, because of the air-conditioning, or the upholstery of a new car. The smell of Brazil is composed of sugar molecules—the hot, sweet smell of baking sugar that wafts from the *padarias*, the bakeries, and coffee shops; and the smell of Gasohol, the potent mix of sugar-derived alcohol and gasoline that powers many of the cars. Atomized in nickel carburetors, the highly volatile alcohol fuel breaks down completely in combustion, leaving only carbon dioxide and water in the air and no poisonous carbon monoxide. Instead of the usual smell of big city pollution, there is the smell of burnt sugar in the air, as though Rio was not merely decadent and unserious, but secretly made of candy floss.

—PAUL RAMBALI, *In the Cities and Jungles of Brazil*

March 29

GORILLAS IN THE MIST

*I*N THE CONFUSION THE GORILLAS SINK AGAIN INTO the dense thicket. Departing, they must cross the path made by the trackers in trying to head them off, and at least fifteen pass in view, including *le gros mâle*. With a sudden roar he rears up, huge-headed, from the green wall, as the nervous Bashi guides yell, "Rongo!"—"Bluffer!"—and the whites fall over one another in the backward surge: the head of the adult gorilla is so enormous that it seems to occupy more than half the width between the shoulder points. But the threat display seems perfunctory and rather bored; *le gros mâle* regards us briefly before turning to give us a good look at his massive side view and the great slope of his crown. Then he drops onto his knuckles once again and shoulders his way into the forest. From neckless neck to waist he is silver white.

—PETER MATTHIESSEN, *African Silences*

INDIAN MARKET

I STEPPED OFF THE BUS IN THE MORNING AT HAMPI Bazaar, a place so bewilderingly strange to Western eyes that I could hardly believe I was seeing it. There was a double row of broken columns, the equivalent of several blocks long. Though now roofless, you'd call it an arcade if you saw it in Italy or at a Californian mission. The columns were huge. They stood maybe as much as five or six feet apart, and, in places, two or three ancient steps still led up to a floor paved with granite slabs, straw, merchandise, and people. It was such a jumble that it took me a few minutes of taking a step and staring, taking another step and staring, to realize that these were people's homes and people's stores. The merchandise—sandals here and pots there, basins, soap, cups, mats, cosmetics, food, fabrics, saris, a thousand items—formed the walls between the columns. Often the merchandise also formed a barrier between the front and back of the stalls. There may have been two families to a stall. Maybe more. There were multitudes crowded between the huge broken columns, sitting about in the streets, walking up and down, staring at the occasional foreigner, no doubt hoping they would buy something; but mostly the vast milling crowd was just living, friendly, curious, and welcoming.

—JAN HAAG, "A VISION OF VIJAYANAGAR,"
Travelers' Tales India

March 31

FOREIGN SOIL

I WANT TO ALWAYS MOVE. THE MOMENT I AM outside the stationed boundaries of home, my body and mind beat intemperately. I celebrate with my whole self. Fear is eliminated from the itinerary. Feet on different soil is a reminder of my courage.

—CHERRILYN ALFONSO, "CELEBRATIONS OF ME"

AN OFFERING IN AN EGYPTIAN PYRAMID

*T*HERE WAS A SUDDEN FLASH, BRIGHTER THAN A thousand suns, as it bounced off the polished walls, caused by the Japanese gentleman letting off a fully thyristorized dedicated AF 200-type flash on top of a Pentax fitted with a lens that seemed more suitable for photographing what lay on the floor at our feet than the actual chamber. Perhaps this was what he was photographing, this unsuitable human offering on the floor.

"Holy hat!" said a fine hard voice that I recognized as that of Rosie, the Girl from the Middle West. "Who in hell laid that? Don't say it was the cop. They got a sign outside, 'No Smoking'. What they want's one saying, 'No Crapping'."

"Well, it wasn't one of us," I said, beginning to suspect that Rosie must have had some more lively incarnation before settling down to life entombment with Haythorn in Peoria, or wherever.

"Let's get out of here," Wanda said, who in some ways is disappointingly sensitive for one who prefers to travel rough. "I think I'm going to be sick."

—ERIC NEWBY, *On the Shores of the Mediterranean*

April 2

PERSIA

*A*LL JOURNEYS IN PERSIA, WHETHER BY ROAD OR air, begin at dawn. Farewells and preparations are made the night before—except that the host rarely fails to speed the parting guest at the gate. Probably more people have seen the dawn in Persia—Europeans at any rate—than in any country in the world. Those who go by road usually want to reach the next stopping place before dark, and the long distance makes an early start necessary, while those who go by air are governed by the desire of the pilots, who want to avoid the heat of the day. Food, water, and the time of starting are the parting conversation for the night. The state of the weather need not worry one, for with the exception of Resht and Pahlavi, two towns on the Caspian Coast, few places get rain for about eight or nine months of the year.

—FRED RICHARDS, *A Persian Journey*

PATH OF GRACE

A WOMAN'S PATH NEED NOT ALWAYS TAKE HER MANY miles from home. It will, however, always invite her to let go of where she's already been, and to be open to the Mystery of where she's going. Grace will be her guide and will ask her to trust in her own wisdom. In this way, a woman's path will invariably lead her back to her true self, and no path is ever more valuable than this.

—SALLY LOWE WHITEHEAD, "A WOMAN'S PATH"

CROSSING BORDERS

*T*HE MEXICAN BORDER WITH THE STATES IS 2,000 miles long. Its very length, and the extremes it has come to represent—First World to Third World, Protestant to Catholic, Anglo-Saxon to Latin—are the source of frequent, more pejorative comparisons: to cross the border has become a metaphysical act in which a traveler passes from credit into debt, from order into chaos, even, as some would have it, from light into dark.

—KATIE HICKMAN, *A Trip to the Light Fantastic*

AT SEA

*A*S WE THREE TRAVELED NORTHWARD ABOARD THE steamer, we watched the Northern Lights which, until this time, I had never seen in such brilliance. As we approached the coast of Norway we sat transfixed at the mag-nificent scenery. Neither Sydney Wilson nor I in all our travels had seen these fjords and cliffs and snow-capped mountains. The water was blue and clear. The land seemed clean and unlittered. On the hilly meadows cattle grazed. Here and there dark forests came down to the sea. But more miracu-  lous than all else were the mountains that were not mountains at all, phantom hills and cliffs through which the eye could pene-trate to valleys and green pastures beyond.

—HARRY DEAN, *The Pedro Gorino* (1929)

April 6

TAKE A WALK

*W*ALKING REMAINS ONE OF THE BEST MEANS OF seeing and interacting with a culture. No boundaries exist, other than the ones that you set for yourself. In the tourist world of packaged tours, seen through closed windows of air-conditioned buses, with carefully prepared cultural events, performed daily for tourists, directed through the conscientious efforts of hired guides, the genuine "travel experience" becomes increasingly rare. But setting out on foot, on your own, is usually all it takes to uncover the sought-after glimpse of life as lived in a strange place.

—JOEL SIMON, "LOST AND FOUND"

A FRENCH MARKET

I HAVE NEVER FOUND A MORE PLEASANT WAY TO GO shopping than to spend two or three hours in a Provençal market. The color, the abundance, the noise, the sometimes eccentric stall-holders, the mingling of smells, the offer of a sliver of cheese here and a mouthful of toast and tapenade there—all these help to turn what began as an errand into a morning's entertainment. An addict could visit a different market every day for several weeks…

—PETER MAYLE, *Encore Provence*

Saudade, the Sweet Yearning

*I*F YOU ARE GOING TO BRAZIL, BE FOREWARNED: WHEN you come back home, if you do, you will have added a few special words to your emotional vocabulary. You will join us in the group that knows the feeling yet cannot explain the meaning of the word...*saudade*. If you can explain it, you've made a poor translation. It has a place of its own, it changes you more than your vocabulary.

If you haven't been somewhere but yearn to see it, you may be getting a glimpse of *saudade*. It means longing for someone or something, more or less in the realm of "I miss you," in English. Yet, it carries more than longing, more than missing. Yearning...a hole carved in one's heart, a feeling which stands on its own as much as it permeates one's whole being.... It simply cannot be translated.

A Brazilian person has *saudade* or feels *saudade*. *Tenho saudades do Brasil* or *Sinto saudades*...portraits of a melancholic yet sweet longing. It transports me there when I say it.

—Neise Cavini Turchin, "Longing,"
Travelers' Tales Brazil

SAME TIME, NEXT YEAR

"*D*ON'T WORRY," HE ADDS, "IT'LL ALL still be here next spring."

The sun goes down, I face the road again, we light up our after-dinner cigars. Keeping the flame alive. The car races forward through a world dissolving into snow and night.

Yes, I agree that's a good thought and it better be so. Or by God there might be trouble. The desert will still be here in the spring. And then comes another thought. When I return will it be the same? Will I be the same? Will anything ever be quite the same again? If I return.

—EDWARD ABBEY (1927–1989)

April 10

FOLLOW YOUR PATH

LIFTING THE LATCH, I STEPPED OUT OF THE garden. In front of me, a path beckoned. It disappeared through trees that covered a sloping bank above a briskly flowing stream. As I walked along the hillside, I could hear below the faint sounds of water slapping against stones. The sun was rapidly fading that afternoon, and I did not have time to follow the path to its end. I could only imagine how it must continue, past the stream and beyond the woods, hurrying toward a mountain lake.

Perhaps I love England most for its paths. They lead across pastures and cultivated fields, over stiles and through gates, into valleys and over hills, along the banks of rivers and canals, beside lakes and ponds, atop mountain ridges and seaside cliffs, past moors, meadows, bogs, and dunes, and through every English garden.

—SUSAN ALLEN TOTH, *My Love Affair with England*

A SEA VOYAGE FROM LIVERPOOL

*L*ET ME ASSURE YOU, MY DEARS . . . THAT GOING to sea is not at all the thing that we have taken it to be. You know how often we have longed for a sea voyage, as the fulfillment of all our dreams of poetry and romance, the realization of our highest conceptions of free, joyous existence.

You remember our ship-launching parties in Maine, when we used to ride to the seaside through dark pine forests, lighted up with the gold, scarlet, and orange tints of autumn. What exhilaration there was, as those beautiful inland bays, one by one, unrolled like silver ribbons before us! And how all our sympathies went forth with the grand new ship about to be launched! How we longed to be with her, and a part of her—to go with her to India, China, or anywhere, so that we might rise and fall on the bosom of that magnificent ocean, and share a part of that glorified existence! That ocean! That blue, sparkling, heaving, mysterious ocean, with all the signs and wonders of heaven emblazoned on its bosom, and another world of mystery hidden beneath its waters!

Alas! what a contrast between all this poetry and the real prose fact of going to sea! No man, the proverb says, is a hero to his *valet de chambre*. Certainly, no poet, no hero, no inspired prophet, ever lost so much on near acquaintance as this same mystic, grandiloquent old Ocean. The one step from the sublime to the ridiculous is never taken with such alacrity as in a sea voyage.

—HARRIET BEECHER STOWE,
Sunny Memories of Foreign Lands (1854)

TAJ MAHAL

*A*S THE ENGLISHMAN LEANED OUT OF THE CARRIAGE he saw first an opal-tinted cloud on the horizon, and, later, certain towers. The mists lay on the ground, so that the

splendour seemed to be floating free of the earth; and the mists rose in the background, so that at no time could everything be seen clearly. Then as the train sped forward, and the mists shifted, and the sun shone upon the mists, the Taj took a hundred new shapes, each perfect and each beyond description. It was the Ivory Gate through which all good dreams come; it was the realization of the gleaming halls of dawn that Tennyson sighs of; it was veritably the "aspiration fixed," the "sigh made stone" of a lesser poet; and over and above concrete comparisons, it seemed the embodiment of all things pure, all things holy, and all things unhappy. That was the mystery of the building.

—RUDYARD KIPLING, *From Sea to Sea* (1897)

THE MASAI MARA GAME RESERVE IN KENYA

*T*HE ANTHILL WAS LIKE A ROUND-TOPPED PEDESTAL as high as the Land Rover, and when we stood up on our seats with our cameras to shoot from the open roof hatches, we were level with our mighty subject and within twenty feet of him. The noon sun brought out the titian tones of the mane that framed his face like a ruff. I gasped over the revealed wonders of this sleeping beauty. He woke on our second tour around him. He stretched, yawned, and suddenly sat up on his pedestal and became a Babylonian statue directly out of the courts of Assurbanipal, except for the missing wings.

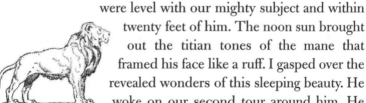

Having spent more than an hour in a royal presence, we were exhausted and exhilarated, a most peculiar state to experience. Apparently one can get a real "high" on lions. I knew that I would recognize that particular lion if ever again I encountered him anywhere in the bush. I had taken him into myself with such visual and emotional intensity as to make him forever a familiar part of me.

—KATHRYN HULME, *Look a Lion in the Eye*

April 14

THE END IN SIGHT

HE NEXT MORNING RAJIV AND I SET OFF THROUGH a mile or so of swamp to a small pond surrounded by trees and filled with rhinos happily blowing bubbles at each other.

They were pretty far away and I asked if we could get a better view. So we headed into the woods.

"Look," Rajiv said, "rhino tracks. We should be able to get a good look right over here!"

We turned right and Rajiv parted the branches in front of him. There, not more than a foot in front of Rajiv's nose, swished the tail of the Great Indian Rhinoceros. Rajiv quietly replaced the branches, turned to me and whispered, "I think we're too close."

—ERIC LURIO, "Buddha is Italian," *Travelers' Tales Nepal*

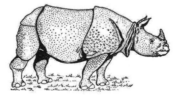

The Colors of Ireland

*I*N THE MORNING, WHEN THE SUN IS SHINING, THAT BEN
is as orange as a clementine. Later it is as green as a ripe lime
and when the clouds return, it fades to a patchwork of smoky
pine and mauve. The white specks scattered across it are grazing sheep. I spend afternoons and mornings trying to burn each
different color into my memory.

The mountains of Connemara are great for hiking. The
bogs, on the other hand, could swallow you whole. As in many
exquisite natural places, danger travels hand in hand with beauty. A few nights after we have settled in, we attend a ceremony in
the church hall commemorating all the people who have been
lost at sea. After reciting the names of the deceased amidst a vigil
of candles, a wreath is sent out to sea. The sea is calm; it obliges
the town's ceremony and accepts the wreath peacefully. By midnight, the winds have whipped up a fury again.

In the morning we venture against the wind to have a look
at the tormented ocean. We decide to take the car and the wipers
slap out a view for us of schoolhouse-size waves; seaweed hurls
itself onto the hood. This becomes the rhythm of our weeks:
days of furious wind and weather interrupted by shocking dis-
plays of moving color. A walk around Aer Lough will reap views
of the twelve pines covered in pink snow, fields of gray rocks and
sienna grass suddenly stunned into mauves and bright yellows,
every possible shade of green, by the sun.

—SARA FRASER, "IN CONNEMARA"

DENMARK

*F*OR SOUL REFRESHMENT AND INSPIRING memories I can think of nothing better for the taut-nerved American than to spend a summer in Denmark. But that summer should begin in mid-April about the time the first stork arrives from Africa and while the ground beneath the tight-budded beaches is still overlaid with a white carpet of star-shaped anemones. In this material age of dubious values and brassy mediocrity, to visit Denmark is something like coming upon a watered garden in an arid earth.

—HUDSON STRODE, *Denmark Is a Lovely Land*

TURKEY

*N*O PART OF THE WORLD CAN BE MORE BEAUTIFUL than the western and southern coasts of Turkey. Their remote valleys break from the treeless plateau, whose oozing snows feed them with harvest wherever the land is flat enough to grow wheat or barley; and to travel in and out of them is like the circumventing of an immense natural fortress, whose walls are precipices with a glacis of fertile stretches before them and whose bastions are toilsome capes that dip, one after another, to the sea.

—FREYA STARK, *Alexander's Path*

April 18

EYES IN EGYPT

I HAD ENCOUNTERED ALL OF THEM BEFORE, occasionally at the doorway to Shaikh Musa's house and sometimes in the guest room when they came in to hand out tea.

 There were times when I had the impression that I had passed them in the lanes of the hamlet, but I was never quite sure. The fault for this lay entirely with me, for neither they nor anyone else in Lataifa wore veils (nor indeed did anyone in the region), but at that time, early in my stay, I was so cowed by everything I had read about Arab traditions of shame and modesty that I barely glanced at them, for fear of giving offence. Later it was I who was shame-stricken, thinking of the astonishment and laughter I must have provoked, walking past them, eyes lowered, never uttering so much as a word of greeting.

—AMITAV GHOOSH, *In an Antique Land*

FINDING CLARITY IN MOUNTAIN AIR

*I*N THE CLEARNESS OF THIS HIMALAYAN AIR, mountains draw near, and in such splendor, tears come quietly to my eyes and cool on my sunburned cheeks. This is not mere soft-mindedness, nor am I all that silly with the altitude. My head has cleared in these weeks free of intrusions —mail, telephones, people and their needs—and I respond to things spontaneously, without defensive or self-conscious  screens. Still, all this feeling is astonishing: not so long ago I could say truthfully that I had not shed a tear in twenty years.

—PETER MATTHIESSEN, *The Snow Leopard*

WHY AM I HERE?

*A*NYONE WHO HAS TRAVELED HAS SAID, IN THE middle of some desert or in a moment of intense alienation in a souk, "Why am I here?" We know that travel is broadening or restorative, or that some inner compulsion we cannot explain prompts us to do it, or that it has to do with escaping from our quotidian lives. But how? Why do we do it? What are the lessons of travel? I have tried to account for those moments of travel ennui or traveler's panic we all have felt: the sheer inability to eat another won ton, the desperate wish to be transported by instantaneous space/time travel into one's own bed.

—DIANE JOHNSON, *Natural Opium*

A CALL TO WIN

*H*E WAS HUGE, FAT, BLIND, AND I WOULD SAY one-legged but I fear that is the addition of my imagination. I passed him every day on my daily jaunt around the Plaza Mayor; he hung out in an arched passageway close to both sun and shade. Over and over again he would shout, at an extraordinarily high pitch, the call to lottery riches: *"¡Para hoy! ¡Para hoy! ¡Me queda El Gordo para hoy!* For today, for today, I've still got the Big One for today!"

The sound still rings in my ears all these many years later, and I often mutter it to myself at odd moments.

—JAMES O'REILLY, "IN SALAMANCA,"
Travelers' Tales Spain

April 22

AROUND THE NEXT BEND

*W*OMEN WHO TRAVEL AS I TRAVEL ARE DREAMERS. Our lives seem to be lives of endless possibility. Like readers of romances, we think that anything can happen to us at any time. We forget that this is not our real life—our life of domestic details, work pressures, attempts and failures at human relations. We keep moving. From anecdote to anecdote, from hope to hope. Around the next bend something new will befall us.

—MARY MORRIS, *Nothing to Declare*

THE CARIOCA SPIRIT

I'LL NEVER FORGET THE FIRST TIME I MET THE CARIOCA spirit face to face. Several years ago, I was sent by a magazine on a dream assignment—to join a samba school in Rio and dance in Carnaval. Since I would be staying on for several months, I rented a small room in Copacabana from Doña Vitória, an elderly widow who rose at dawn every day to bake cookies for high-society parties. One night, when we were discussing whether she should leave the door unlocked for me, I muttered something about having found a new boyfriend, and was perhaps—well—not coming home. For a moment she looked confused, then suddenly she threw out her arms and hugged me. "Ah, *querida*, go! Have fun, eat, dance, laugh, make love! Life is so short!" In that brief moment, the joy of her Carioca spirit blazed through me, and, as I shut the door behind me, I felt somehow I'd been blessed.

—PAMELA BLOOM, *Brazil Up Close*

April 24

AT THE POST

*I*NEEDED TO MAIL BOOKS HOME FROM JAIPUR. AT the post office I discovered that I had to find a tailor to sew the books inside a cloth bag since they do not use boxes. Mission completed, I thought, back at the post office within an hour. Then I discovered that I needed my name imbedded on hot wax at the seams so that it would be obvious (for insurance purposes) if the bag had been opened. Sensing my exasperation, the clerk pointed his head, smiled, motioned me to his seat in the chair at the window and went outside to find some wax. Fortunately, the first customer at the window spoke English. He wanted three stamps, which cost a total of one rupee. His smallest coin was a two rupee piece. I gave him the stamps and he left the two rupee piece even though I had no change. My next customer spoke no English. He also wanted three stamps and didn't seem to have the right change. I gave him the stamps at no charge since I had an extra rupee from the first customer.

The postal clerk came back with a foil-wrapped piece of chocolate with the name Heller embossed on it. He pointed to a general store where I bought a red candle. The store owner dripped the wax along the seams of the bag and, as it turned out, onto the covers of the books. I have red sealing wax on my book jackets as a memento of the day I worked in the Jaipur post office.

—CAROL LEVY, "VAGABOND," *Travelers' Tales India*

THE ONCE REMOTE TIP OF JAMAICA

*N*O MATTER HOW DEVELOPED NEGRIL BECOMES, it still looks like a sleepy little town. Alligators hide in the almost impenetrable mangrove swamps that give no hint of the crystal waters that lay beyond them. You can watch, and feel, clouds of mosquitoes descending—no matter how much pesticide the town has employed to exterminate them—right along with the spectacular sunsets at Rick's Café. Or you can allow the velvet cloak of the night to wrap itself around you like a soft blanket as you sit back and do nothing but drink a Red Stripe beer and listen to waves crashing against the cliffs. It's a sensory feast for all to discover.

And to me it's beautiful, still paradise after all these years.

—SUZANNE MCFAYDEN-SMITH, "PARADISE"

April 26

ONE WITH THE LAND

WE STEP INTO THE STREET AND MY FRIEND DAVID Shahar, whose chest is large, takes a deep breath and advises me to do the same. The air, the very air, is thought-nourishing in Jerusalem, the Sages themselves said so. I am prepared to believe it. I know that it must have special properties. The delicacy of the light also affects me. I look downward toward the Dead Sea, over broken rocks and small houses with bulbous roofs. The color of these is that of the ground itself, and on this strange deadness the melting air presses with an almost human weight. Something intelligible, something metaphysical is communicated by these colors. The universe interprets itself before your eyes in the openness of the rock-jumbled valley ending in dead water. Elsewhere you die and disintegrate. Here you die and mingle.

—SAUL BELLOW, *To Jerusalem and Back*

AN AMAZONIAN SHAVE

*A*BOUT 2 P.M., WE PULLED UP AT A BIG SHAKY
river house, where a warmhearted man named Jibuzcio
came striding down an elevated walkway to meet us. His wife
and six children soon joined him. They invited us to stay. When
Dana and I had bathed and shampooed, I asked Jibuzcio if he
had a razor. "Sim," he said, and he produced a rusty old razor
blade fastened with thread to a Popsicle stick.

"Will you shave me?" I said to Jibuzcio. "Sim," he said, and
in no time I was seated in the main room of the house with my
head back. For fifteen minutes, Jibuzcio scratched away at my
beard, throwing the scratching out the window into the river. At
one point I asked him if he'd built his own house and when.
He'd built it, he said, but he couldn't remember quite when.
"Could be 25 years ago."

A few minutes later—still with my head back—I happened to
glance at a rafter which was deeply inscribed with the numbers
"27 4 55." It had to be a date, and, after a few seconds, it dawned
on me that it was today's date, but 27 years ago. I waited a minute
and said cryptically, "Your home is 27 years old, not 25," and I
pointed at the inscription. He peered up at it for a few seconds
and excitedly called to his family. All of them rushed in and stood
gazing into the rafters at the numbers. The house was 27 years
old today, and the whole place instantly took on a birthday
atmosphere   and I didn't get so much as a nick from my shave.

—DON STARKELL, *Paddle to the Amazon*

April 28

THE MEANING OF TRAVEL

*S*OME VERY WISE WRITERS HAVE DEFINED TRAVEL AS "the exploration of inner space—the losing of the self in order to find oneself"; "a pursuit of rootlessness"; "the recurrent human desire to drop our lives and walk out of them"; "to leave home where we impersonate ourselves and to become whomever we please." Paul Fussell wrote in *Abroad* about the travels of D. H. Lawrence: "What he really saw in other things and places was the infinite."

—DAVID YEADON, *The Back of Beyond*

THE NEVER-ENDING JOURNEY

*T*RAVEL, AT HEART, IS JUST A QUICK WAY TO KEEP our minds mobile and awake. As Santayana, the heir to Emerson and Thoreau, wrote, "There is wisdom in turning as often as possible from the familiar to the unfamiliar; it keeps the mind nimble; it kills prejudice, and it fosters humor." Romantic poets inaugurated an era of travel because they were the great apostles of open eyes. Buddhist monks are often vagabonds, in part because they believe in wakefulness. And if travel is like love, it is, in the end, mostly because it's a heightened state of awareness, in which we are mindful, receptive, undimmed by familiarity and ready to be transformed. That is why the best trips, like the best love affairs, never really end.

—PICO IYER, "WHY WE TRAVEL"

GET LOST

*E*XPLORATION IS NOTHING MORE THAN A FORAY into the unknown, and a four-year-old child, wandering about alone in the department store, fits the definition as well as the snow-blind man wandering across the Khyber Pass. The explorer is the person who is lost.

—TIM CAHILL, *Jaguars Ripped My Flesh*

FOREIGN FRUIT

*W*e found many that had eaten the durian, and they all spoke of it with a sort of rapture. They said that if you could hold your nose until the fruit was in your mouth a sacred joy would suffuse you from head to foot that would make you oblivious to the smell of the rind, but that if your grip slipped and you caught the smell of the rind before the fruit was in your mouth, you would faint. There is a fortune in that rind. Some day somebody will import it into Europe and sell it for cheese.

MARK TWAIN, *More Tramps Abroad* (1897)

PHILAE, THE ISLE OF EGYPT

*P*ERHAPS THE GENERAL MONOTONY OF THE scenery on the Nile gives it a peculiar beauty; but I think it would be called beautiful anywhere, even among the finest scenes in Italy. It brought forcibly to my mind, but seemed to me far more lovely than, the Lake Maggiore, with the beautiful Isola Bella and Isola Madre. It is entirely unique, a beautiful *lusus naturae*, a little island about a thousand feet long and four hundred broad, rising in the center of a circular bay, which appears to be cut off from the river, and forms a lake surrounded by dark sandstone rocks; carpeted with green to the water's edge, and covered with columns, propylons, and towers, the ruins of a majestic temple. A sunken wall encircles it on all sides.

—JOHN LLOYD STEPHENS,
Incidents of Travel in Egypt (1837)

Go Your Own Way

*T*RAVEL IS A PERSONAL THING, LIKE RAISING A FAMILY, and to reduce it to a science, as the tour operators have done, is to make it meaningless. It is too delicate to be homogenized, sterilized, and rendered so predictable that one may as well remain in one's living room. The notion of travel is based upon a desire to escape, at least temporarily, from the familiar, the known, the totally secure. Travel demands more determination than courage; a determination to participate and not to play the role of an observer. The airlines have come to refer to travelers as "seats" and hotels refer to them as "beds"; this offends me but it shows how far down the road to mass manipulation we have drifted.

—CASKIE STINNETT, *Grand and Private Pleasures*

May 4

THE PILGRIM'S PATH

*I*F YOU CHOSE TO MAKE THE PILGRIMAGE IN THE authentic manner, by walking it or riding it on horseback, you still take the original track, along which tens of millions of other pilgrims have passed before you, a road where cobbles have been rubbed as soft as sea pebbles, rutted by Roman carts, polished by passing horseshoes. You see exactly the same sights, feel the same pains, as generations of previous pilgrims—men like John of Gaunt and Saint Francis of Assisi, women like Chaucer's formidable Wife of Bath.

—WILLIAM DALRYMPLE, "WALKING TO SANTIAGO"

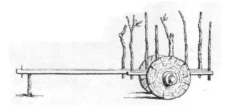

LONDON, ENGLAND

*L*ONDON IS ENCHANTING. I STEP OUT UPON A
tawny coloured magic carpet, it seems, & get carried into
beauty without raising a finger. The nights are amazing, with all
the white porticoes & broad silent avenues. And people pop in
& out, lightly, divertingly, like rabbits; & I look down
Southampton Row, wet as a seal's back or red & yellow with
sunshine, & watch the omnibus going & coming, & hear the old
crazy organs. One of these days I will write about London &
how it takes up the private life & carries it on, without any effort.
Faces passing lift up my mind; prevent it from settling.

—VIRGINIA WOOLF, *Diary*

May 6

MY LIST

*A*ND SO I LOOK FORWARD TO MY NEXT JOURNEY. I don't know where it will be yet, but I do have a long list. Whenever someone tells me about a great spot that I must check out I say, "I'll have to put that on my list." I just know that no matter where I go in the world, traveling renews my faith in humankind, as well as in myself. It's a journey of remembrance back to my original self, the one who is wholly connected to all beings and nature. It's a journey that rediscovers what's really important, ultimately.

—BARBARA SANSONE, "UNDER THE MANGO TREE,"
The Road Within

THE PEKING-TO-PARIS MOTOR CHALLENGE

I AM READY AND WILLING TO CONQUER ANOTHER long-distance rally. I can't afford it, but my attitude about money has changed, too: it's out there, lots of it. Just because I don't have any now doesn't mean I won't somehow find a way to afford an expensive journey. The trick for next time is to figure out how to bring along my husband, maybe even my kids. We'll head for one of those places on this incredible globe where geography, history, and humanity combine in awe-inspiring synergy.

A place like Greece.

We'll drive up a steep, narrow road. The tall, straight cypress and craggy, crooked olive trees will climb the hillside beside us. The warm air will smell of dust, oregano, and our own exhaust. When the road suddenly falls away as we crest the summit, we'll glimpse far below us an ancient abode of the gods: tumbled marble and titled columns lying silent at the base of a high, volcanic mountain. A phosphorescent sea will ripple green and blue on the horizon, as we drive to the heart of the world.

—GENEVIEVE OBERT, *Prince Borghese's Trail*

May 8

THE JOY OF JET LAG

*A*FTER ARRIVING IN DUBLIN FROM SAN FRANCISCO I am experiencing a very strange jet lag. Four nights now without a wink of sleep between midnight and five A.M., perhaps in part because I'm sharing a bed with my three-year-old daughter, Alanna, in a separate room as we try to get her on an Ireland schedule. The first three nights Alanna and I lay awake together most of the night, telling stories in the dark, shuffling about beneath the blankets, cuddling as the rain blew about the trees. Possibly I'm wide awake because these moments are so precious. Watching that glorious, innocent face on the pillow next to me, when Alanna's finally asleep, is worth hours of sleeplessness. I'm aware that I may never again have such moments, where we share a bed alone, and she is secure with her daddy as she dreams of penguins and fairies. The trip has been worth it for that alone. It is such a reward to get a pure kiss in the morning when she wants to wake me up so she can get some breakfast. It's new to me, and a real joy.

—LARRY HABEGGER, "ON IRISH TIME"

MANAGUA, NICARAGUA

THE MOST ATTRACTIVE FEATURE OF Managua is the habit its people have, in the evening, of bringing their rocking-chairs out on to the pavement. It is impossible to walk more than a few yards down a street, for at almost every front door one is stopped by a family circle, all bobbing up and down in their chairs, and forcing one to step out into the traffic. But one doesn't complain, for it is a friendly and aesthetic custom.

—NICHOLAS WOLLASTON, *Red Rumba*

May 10

ETHIOPIA

*T*HE MAGNIFICENT SCENERY LIGHT-ened the fatigue in no small way: for there can be no doubt that it is less tiring to march through a beautiful country than over a dead flat, although most of the men may be unconscious, or but half-conscious, of the reason for this difference. They swore at the mountain passes, while actually enjoying their grandeur. "They tell us this is a table-land," exclaimed one of the 33d, in climbing up the Alaji ascent. "If it is, they have turned the table upside down, and we are scrambling up and down the legs."

—CLEMENTS R. MARKHAM,
A History of the Abyssinian Expedition (1869)

KATHMANDU

*T*HERE ARE MANY THINGS ONE "SHOULD SEE" in this valley, but I secretly resent being bossed by guidebooks and am therefore a slipshod tourist. To me the little statue that one unexpectedly discovers down an alleyway, and impulsively responds to, means much more than the temple one had been instructed to admire for erudite and probably incomprehensible reasons.

—DERVLA MURPHY, *The Waiting Land*

May 12

AMAZON FOREST

*T*HE FOREST OF THE AMAZON IS NOT MERELY TREES and shrubs. It is not land. It is another element. Its inhabitants are arboreal; they have been fashioned for life in that medium as fishes to the sea and birds to the air. Its green apparition is persistent as the sky is and the ocean. In months of travel it is the horizon which the traveler cannot reach, and its unchanging surface, merged through distance into a mere reflector of the day, a brightness or a gloom, in his immediate vicinity breaks into a complexity of green surges; then one day the voyager sees land at last and is released from it.

—H. M. TOMLINSON,
The Sea and the Jungle (1912)

LAS VEGAS

*T*OWARDS THE END OF MY TRIP, MY MOTHER CAME to visit. We drove down Tropicana Avenue and hit the Strip at the New York-New York Hotel. It was night and the lights shook like aspens. We drove past the pink *porte cochre* of Caesar's Palace. We watched the fake volcano going off.

"Isn't this just marvelous," my mum said, giggling with pleasure.

We ate double-decker ice creams among the cords of brilliant neon and below us, invisible to the eye, flowed the thick water of the silver stream. Thomas Lynch, the poet undertaker, told me his aunt always used to say that life is wonderful if you can resist temptation and wonderful if you can't. That night we watched the smudge of traffic and we felt our best selves. Mum didn't notice the vacant lots, the dust of building sites, the drunks slumped at the bus stops. She saw what Vegas wanted her to see. "It's so enormous and tacky and beautiful," she said.

And she was right. It was.

—MELANIE MCGRATH, *Motel Nirvana*

May 14

NO BARRIERS HERE

*I*HAD FORGOTTEN ABOUT THAT LIGHT. I HAD forgotten the numberless evenings I'd sat on the same terrace, alone or with friends, watching it change, wrapped in that expanse of rose gold light. That night, with the heavy labor of cleaning over at last, I could feel something inside begin to loosen, the chronic knot I never knew I had until I came to Greece, and it disappeared. This night on the terrace I could feel it loosen, thread by thread, so that it seemed as if I had just swollen up by taking in some of what was around me, and what was around me had taken in some of me—a kind of psychic orgasm, where there was no separation, no barrier between figure and ground. As if the universe had been trying to tell me something: that in reality there were no barriers, no barriers at all and most of all no barriers to light, no more to learn about.

—NANCY RAEBURN, *Mykonos*

GULF OF SUEZ

*T*HE BEAUTY OF THE GULF OF SUEZ—AND SURELY it is most beautiful—has never received full appreciation from the traveler. He is in too much of a hurry to arrive or to depart, his eyes are too ardently bent on England or India for him to enjoy the exquisite corridor of tinted mountains and radiant water. He is too much occupied with his own thoughts to realize that here, here and nowhere else, is the vestibule between the Levant and the Tropics.

—E. M. FORESTER, *Pharos and Pharillon*

JUST A MATTER OF TIME

I SAT IN THE DELHI AIRPORT AND WATCHED THE BIG electric clock in the departure hall that tells passengers when to board. I thought I imagined that time was moving in fits and starts: 1:12 A.M. for fifteen minutes, then 1:27 for another twenty, 1:47…. Closer inspection revealed that the clock was not plugged in, and its digits were being flipped manually by a little man in gray overalls whenever the mood took him.

—JONAH BLANK, *Arrow of the Blue-Skinned God*

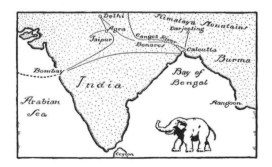

GOODBYES

*T*HE LORRY ARRIVED AFTER BREAKFAST. WE embraced for the last time. I said, "Go in peace," and they answered together, "Remain in the safe keeping of God, *Umbarak.*" Then they scrambled up on to a pile of petrol drums beside a Palestinian refugee in oil-stained dungarees. A few minutes later they were out of sight round a corner. I was glad when Codrai took me to the aerodrome at Sharja. As the plane climbed over the town and swung out above the sea I knew how it felt to go into exile.

—WILFRED THESIGER, *Arabian Sands*

PILGRIMAGE

*F*or in their hearts doth Nature stir them so,
    Then People long on pilgrimage to go,
  And palmers to be seeking foreign strands,
    To distant shrines renowned in sundry lands.

—GEOFFREY CHAUCER,
The Canterbury Tales (1380s)

UGANDA

I HAVE TRAVELLED THROUGH TROPICAL FORESTS IN Cuba and India, and had often before admired their enchanting, yet sinister luxuriance. But the forests of Uganda, for magnificence, for variety of form and colour, for profusion of brilliant life—plant, bird, insect, reptile, beast—for the vast scale and awful fecundity of the natural processes that are beheld at work, eclipsed, and indeed effaced, all previous impressions. One becomes, not without a secret sense of aversion, the spectator of an intense convulsion of life and death. Reproduction and decay are locked struggling in infinite embraces. In this glittering equatorial slum huge trees jostle one another for room to live; slender growths stretch upwards—as it seems in agony—towards sunlight and life. The soil bursts with irrepressible vegetations. Every victor, trampling on the rotting mould of exterminated antagonists, soars aloft, only to encounter another host of aerial rivals, to be burdened with masses of parasitic foliage, smothered in the glorious blossoms of creepers, laced and bound and interwoven with interminable tangles of vines and trailers. Birds are as bright as butterflies; butterflies are as big as birds…. The telegraph-wire runs northwards to Gondoroko through this vegetable labyrinth. Even its poles had broken into bud.

—SIR WINSTON CHURCHILL, *My African Journey* (1908)

THE AMERICAN DESERT

*T*HERE IS SOMETHING DEEPLY APPEALING ABOUT ancient landscapes that silently endure all manner of geologic chaos. This unearthly patience of the desert is what has drawn generations of adventures, outlaws, poets, painters, and writers to its secret Bedouin heart. They come to soak up the fierce romance of desert, wind, and sun. The timeless duration of this land lends itself freely to the thoughts of those who wish to meditate on its history and vistas.

After a recent visit from my younger sister Maggie, herself a reluctant Easterner, she wrote: "The desert must echo something of eternity with its restful intensity, for I can pull the memory of it into my mind's eye and it calms me. Funny, but the desert seems to be an oasis for me."

The desert will do that to you. It is as if an enormous and moving consolation has been made out of emptiness and wonder. And there are so many things to wonder at in the Southwest.

—SEAN O'REILLY,
Travelers' Tales American Southwest

EIMEO, TAHITI

*O*N THE LOFTY AND BROKEN PINNACLES, WHITE massive clouds were piled up, which formed an island in the blue sky, as Eimeo itself did in the blue ocean. The island, with the exception of one small gateway, is completely encircled by a reef. At this distance a narrow, but well-defined brilliantly white line was alone visible, where the waves first encountered the wall of coral. The mountains rose abruptly out of the glassy expanse of the lagoon included within this narrow white line, outside which the heaving waters of the ocean were dark-colored. The view was striking: it may aptly be compared to a framed engraving, where the frame represents the breakers, the marginal paper the smooth lagoon, and the drawing the island itself.

—CHARLES DARWIN, *Journal During the Voyage of H.M.S. Beagle* (1832–1836)

ALPINE JOURNEY

*W*ILDFLOWERS DAZZLED THE EYES AND NOSE. Flocks of fuchsia finches eschered with yellow butterflies in the sparkling mountain sky. Cows, like four-legged vacationers, were arriving by train to summer in the high Alpine pastures. In September, I was told, they'd be brought down again, cowbells clanging, their horns and necks bedecked with flower chains, to join a day of music and merrymaking in the villages.

Mountains are great shapers of character, it is said. And great stimuli for engineers, too—the challenge of living in such difficult terrain has goaded the Swiss to tackle almost every peak with a cog railway, tramway, or tunnel. But it was the valleys and canyons that piqued my interest: the narrow gorges and wild cataracts of the Danube's scenic tributary, the En.

—PAMELA MICHAEL, "SWISS SQUEEZE,"
The Gift of Rivers

A VISION IN THE DESERT

*B*EAUTY IS A POOR STANDARD BY WHICH TO JUDGE human beings but how could people who look like that not be beautiful inside as well. What flair! What sense of color and design! What magnanimous display of self for the delight of others! First, the turbans. Purple red gold black silk, tied so that they had a slightly triangular shape lending the forces beneath a Pharonic cast. Next, a long-sleeved smock made of thick white cotton drill, embroidered in minute stitches of every color— purples and reds dominating—edged in a gold or silver, tight fitting until gathered beneath the breast to flare at narrow hips; the sleeves pushed up into wrinkles at the wrist. Beneath the smocks, white lawn *dhotis*, one of the oldest forms of dress in the world, were tucked into pink-, red- and black-striped nylon socks which disappeared into high-heeled leather clogs decorated with brass studs, the toes curling backwards into Sinbad points. They hung around together in groups like adolescent boys anywhere, shy and giggling one minute, swaggering the next. And, in among the riot of color, groups of women in black wool and silver, black *omis* swelling out like jub-sails strode past whitewashed walls.

—ROBYN DAVIDSON, *Desert Places*

BANGKOK

*F*ROM THE VERY BEGINNING I WAS CHARMED BY Bangkok, and I propose to be aggressively syrupy about it in the most buckeye travelogue manner. I liked its polite, gentle, handsome people, its temples, flowers, and canals, the relaxed and peaceful rhythm of life there. Apart from its shrill and tumultuous central thoroughfare swarming with Chinese and Indian bazaars, it struck me as the most soothing metropolis I had thus far seen in the East. Its character is complex and inconsistent; it seems at once to combine the Hannibal, Missouri, of Mark Twain's boyhood with Beverly Hills, the Low Countries, and Chinatown. You pass from populous, glaring streets laden with traffic into quiet country lanes paralleled by canals out of a Dutch painting; a tree-shaded avenue of pretentious mansions set in wide lawns abruptly becomes a bustling row of shops and stalls, then melts into a sunny village of thatched huts among which water buffalo graze. The effect is indescribably pleasing; your eye constantly discovers new vistas, isolated little communities around every corner tempting you to explore them.

—S. J. PERELMAN, *Westward Ha!*

PASSING FOR A LOCAL

M Y LAST EVENINGS IN ALEXANDRIA I TRIED TO lose myself, to become one of the crowd. I knew it was a slightly ridiculous illusion. But I am still proud of the fact that I used to walk through Montmartre at night without being accosted by a single tout, that is to say, without sticking out as a stranger. Alexandria isn't Paris; still, it's on the sea, which gives its character a certain accessibility. I got close enough to taste being part of it—the excitement of being someone else, utterly removed from the fears and from the securities of our world.

—HANS KONIG, *A New Yorker in Egypt*

SAVORY LANGUAGE

*A*T NIGHT IN GERMANY, WHEN YOU PACE UP AND down the platform, there is always someone to explain things to you. The round heads and the long heads get together in a cloud of vapor and all the wheels are taken apart and put together again. The sound of the language seems more penetrating than other tongues, as if it were food for the brain, substantial, nourishing, appetizing. Glutinous particles detach themselves and they dissipate slowly, months after the voyage, like a smoker exhaling a fine stream of smoke through his nostrils after he has taken a drink of water. The word *gut* is the longest lasting word of all. "*Es war gut!*" says someone, and his gut rumbles in my bowels like a rich pheasant. Surely nothing is better than to take a train when all the inhabitants are asleep and to drain from their open mouths the rich succulent morsels of their unspoken tongue. When every one sleeps the mind is crowded with events; the mind travels in a swarm, like summer flies that are sucked along by the train.

—HENRY MILLER, *Black Spring*

ALASKAN REVERENCE

ONE NIGHT WHEN A HEAVY RAINSTORM WAS BLOW-ING I unwittingly caused a lot of wondering excitement among the whites as well as the superstitious Indians. Being anxious to see how the Alaska trees behave in storms and hear the songs they sing, I stole quietly away through the gray drenching blast to the hill back of the town, without being observed. Night was falling when I set out and it was pitch dark when I reached the top. The glad, rejoicing storm in glorious voice was singing through the woods, noble compensation for mere body discomfort. But I wanted a fire, a big one, to see as well as hear how the storm and trees were behaving.... Of the thousands of camp-fires I have elsewhere built none was just like this one, rejoicing in triumphant strength and beauty in the heart of the rain-laden gale. It was wonderful—the illuminated rain and clouds mingled together and the trees glowing against the jet background, the colors of the mossy, lichened trunks with sparkling streams pouring down the furrows of the bark, and the gray-bearded old patriarchs bowing low and chanting in passionate worship!

—JOHN MUIR, *Travels in Alaska* (1879)

THE END OF A JOURNEY

*T*HE SOUTHERN HORIZON WAS EMPTY—SOMEWHERE below that blue distance lay the purple mountains of Crete—lost for many years to come; but I knew even then that something of its spell would stay with me forever. Perhaps I would come back again one day. Perhaps, after all, life didn't

always move away in a straight relentless line from happiness, like the wake of this little ship streaming away astern in a froth of cream and jade on the blue-black water.

I turned away, and looked forward. A little ahead on the starboard side a green island rose out of the sea, shimmering in the early morning sun. It was Milos, and a year-old memory stirred

in me. Once again I was nearing the Greek mainland from the south, once again I was slipping past one of her quiet welcoming outposts.

I wasn't traveling away from happiness at all. I had simply come full circle.

—MARY CHUBB, *City in the Sand*

VIRUNGA NATIONAL PARK, EAST AFRICA

I DIDN'T SEE ANYTHING INITIALLY, BUT WHEN I LOOKED toward one of the noises, I could see a big patch of black in with the green, then another and another. We took a few steps forward and soon branches were crackling all around us. There were gorillas everywhere, even little ones in the trees above.

My impulse was to back right out of there, but the gorillas' countenance was so gentle that they soon put me at ease. They were so obviously gentle and so aware of their surroundings that I felt totally trusting of them. "No one who looks into a gorilla's eyes—intelligent, gentle, vulnerable—can remain unchanged," the naturalist George Schaller once wrote, and I understood what he meant. They looked like they might start speaking if you stayed long enough. But I could also tell that after a while we were being intrusive and bothersome by constantly following them. Finally the silverback went into an area of thick brush where we couldn't follow, and growled a few times as if to say, "Okay, the session's over. Get out of here."

We left reluctantly, looking back often as we walked in silence through the depths of green leaves and yellow light. When we stepped back out of the forest, it was like stepping out of a dream.

—KEVIN KERTSCHER, *Africa Solo*

CHANGING FRAMES

YOU SEE THINGS VACATIONING ON A MOTORCYCLE in a way that is completely different from any other. In a car you're always in a compartment, and because you're used to it you don't realize that through that car window everything you see is just more TV. You're a passive observer and it is all moving by you boringly in a frame.

On a cycle the frame is gone. You're completely in contact with it all. You're in the scene, not just watching it anymore, and the sense of presence is overwhelming. That concrete whizzing by five inches below your foot is the real thing, the same stuff you walk on, it's right there, so blurred you can't focus on it, yet you can put your foot down and touch it anytime, and the whole thing, the whole experience is never removed from immediate consciousness.

—ROBERT PIRSIG,
Zen and the Art of Motorcycle Maintenance

COSTA DEL SOL

*A*S YOU REACH THE *MIRADOR* ON THE CLIFF OVER the glistening sea, you hear the characteristic sounds of Andalucía: the screech and twitter of swallows overhead, faint high-pitched voices from the street, a distant strain of flamenco, the haunting pan-pipe of the itinerant knife grinder, the muffled whump of the Mediterranean on the rocks below, and the church bell from the plaza chiming the hour. Before the dying chime has faded, a motorcycle with no muffler rends the reverie and a pair of jackhammers begin their daily assault on the remains of the old house across the street. It is morning on the Costa del Sol.

—ALLEN JOSEPHS, *White Wall of Spain*

June 1

VALLEY OF THE ROSES

*A*LL MY LIFE I HAVE HEARD OF BULGARIA'S legendary Valley of the Roses; I imagined it to be a sort of botanic gardens, carefully tended parterres, a summer afternoon's stroll. But it is a whole region, twenty miles wide, a hundred miles long, a pink province; at once a tradition and a livelihood: a whole world of its own into which people are born, and where they live and work and die, set a little apart from the rest, and as it were becalmed in fragrance.

It seems there are only a few weeks—in June, when the roses reach their apotheosis. Rose culture demands not only the precise moment of the year, but the exact moment of the day—sunrise. The flowers must be gathered while the dew is still on them, before the heat of the sun had drawn out all their perfume. Today is the first of June. Now is "the time, and the place."

—LESLEY BLANCH, *Under a Lilac-Bleeding Star*

A PASSION FOR CLIMBING

*B*Y THE AGE OF EIGHTEEN CLIMBING WAS THE ONLY thing I cared about: work, school, friendships, career plans, sex, sleep—all were made to fit around my climbing or, more often, neglected out-right. In 1974 my preoccupation intensified further still. The pivotal event was my first Alaskan expedition, a month-long trip with six companions to the Arrigetch  Peaks, a knot of slender granite towers possessed of a severe, haunting beauty. One June morning at 2:30 A.M., after climbing for twelve straight hours, I pulled up onto the summit of a mountain called Xanadu. The top was a disconcertingly narrow fin of rock, likely the highest point in the whole range. And ours were the first boots ever to step upon it. Far below, the spikes and slabs of the surrounding peaks glowed orange, as if lit from within, in the eerie, nightlong dusk of the arctic summer. A bitter wind screamed across the tundra from the Beaufort Sea, turning my hands to wood. I was as happy as I'd ever been in my life.

—JON KRAKAUER, *Eiger Dreams*

June 3

A SPIRITUAL GEOGRAPHY

*T*HE HIGH PLAINS, THE BEGINNING OF THE DESERT West, often act as a crucible for those who inhabit them. Like Jacob's angel, the region requires that you wrestle with it before it bestows a blessing. This can mean driving through a snowstorm on icy roads, wondering whether you'll have to pull over and spend the night in your car, only to emerge under tag ends of clouds into a clear sky blazing with stars. Suddenly you know what you're seeing: the earth has turned to face the center of the galaxy, and many more stars are visible than the ones we usually see on our wing of the spiral.

Or a vivid double rainbow marches to the east, following the wild summer storm that nearly blew you off the road. The storm sky is gunmetal gray, but to the west the sky is peach streaked with crimson. The land and sky of the West often fill what Thoreau termed our "need to witness our limits transgressed." Nature, in Dakota, can indeed be an experience of the holy.

—KATHLEEN NORRIS, *Dakota*

VENICE

I HAVE BEEN BETWEEN HEAVEN AND EARTH SINCE OUR arrival at Venice. The heaven of it is ineffable. Never had I touched the skirts of so celestial a place. The beauty of the architecture, the silver trails of water up between all that gorgeous colour and carving, the enchanting silence, the moonlight, the music, the gondolas—I mix it all up together, and maintain that nothing is like it, nothing to equal it, not a second Venice in the world. Do you know when I came first I felt as if I could never go away. But now comes the earth side. Robert, after sharing the ecstasy, grows uncomfortable, and nervous, and unable to eat or sleep.... Alas for these mortal Venices—so exquisite and so bilious!

—ELIZABETH BARRETT BROWNING,
LETTER TO MISS MITFORD (1851)

June 5

FOLLOWING THE SINAI SUN

THE EARTH IS SO SAMELY, THAT YOUR EYES TURN towards heaven—towards heaven, I mean in sense of sky. You look to the Sun, for he is your task-master, and by him you know the measure of the work that you have done, and the measure of the work that remains for you to do. He comes when you strike your tent in the early morning, and then, for the first hour of the day, as you move forward on your camel, he stands at your near side, and makes you know that the whole day's toil is before you; then for a while, and a long while, you see him no more, for you are veiled and shrouded, and dare not look upon the greatness of his glory, but you know where he strides over head, by the touch of his flaming sword. No words are spoken, but your Arabs moan, your camels sigh, your skin glows, your shoulders ache, and for sights you see the pattern and the web of the silk that veils your eyes, and the glare of the outer light. Time labors on—your skin glows, your shoulders ache, your Arabs moan, your camels sign, and you see the same pattern in the silk, and the same glare of light beyond; but conquering Time marches on, and by and by the descending sun has compassed the heaven, and now softly touches your right arm, and throws your lank shadow over the sand right along on the way for Persia.

—A.W. KINGLAKE, *Eothen* (1844)

ANDALUCIAN SHORE

*B*EYOND ESTEPONA THERE WAS A PLEASANT BEACH, with a cover between two spurs of rock, one of which jutted out to sea. I thought I would bathe from these rocks, but a *guardia civil* emerged from a hut on the road above me and told me that this beach belonged to an English general at Gibraltar, who allowed no one to bathe there. People might only bathe from the other side of the further rocks. It seemed that the general owned about half a kilometer of beach. I asked if I might swim out from further down the shore and land on the rocks of the general; the guard said no, the general did not permit that one landed on his rocks. Does the general own the sea too? I asked. Yes, the sea also was the general's. For how far out? For two kilometers, replied the guard—further than I would wish to swim, and I agreed.

[I] had to bathe further down. But it was a pleasant bathe, in that warm and scintillating afternoon sea. It was, I reflected, one of my last Mediterranean bathes, for it was only about twenty-five miles to the Straits, the Pillars of Hercules, where the known world ended and the dark bottomless void of the misty Ocean began.

—ROSE MACAULAY, *Fabled Shore*

June 7

A BIRD'S EYE VIEW OF TURKEY

*B*EFORE WE VENTURED TO DIVE INTO THE DARK and mysterious labyrinths of Stamboul, we thought it best to take our usual precaution, that of ascending some tower to observe well how the land lies, and to take a fair departure. We have always found, by so doing when we first enter any foreign city and when we are about to leave it, that we obtain an indelible impression of its general location, form, and extent, the proportionate size and peculiar appearance of its principal monuments and other prominent features. I would recommend all young and persevering travelers to adopt this practice.

—SARAH ROGERS HAIGHT,
Letters from the Old World (1840)

June 8

SAVORING A MEMORY

I HAVE A COLOR PHOTOGRAPH OF MYSELF ON MY WALL
in New York that was taken by a friend. I am in our house in
St. Sébastien, in the kitchen. The sunlight, even indoors, is
intense, rich. I am holding a head of lettuce in my hand. I am
holding it before me, and I am looking at it and smiling. It is lettuce I have grown myself, in my own garden. It is one of those
soft, densely packed heads, the leaves of which you find in salads in most bistros in France. We probably ate it with our lunch
that day—at least I hope we did—with a little olive oil and perhaps a splash of lemon. And perhaps with it, some slices of
tomato, bleeding with summer, also taken from the garden. And
since the photograph was taken by a friend, it's certain that he,
and maybe some others, shared that meal with us, seated around
our long wooden table, the windows thrown open, letting the
summer air stream in. Wine, bread, cheese, water, meat, salad
before us all.

—RICHARD GOODMAN, *French Dirt*

TAKE A TRIP

I THINK IT WAS JUNG WHO POINTED OUT THERE IS a big difference between falling and diving. At the beginning of this trip I was falling, I think; a figure at the mercy of gravity and whatever passing object I could grab on the way down. Like maps or friendly cafés or people who spoke English. Now, even though my form is far from perfect, I am better able to dive into new waters, leaving behind barely a splash as I enter.

—ALICE STEINBACH, *Without Reservations*

DANGER IS AN APHRODISIAC

*L*OVE THRIVES ESPECIALLY WELL IN EXOTIC locales. When the senses are heightened because of stress, novelty, or fear, it's much easier to become a mystic or feel ecstasy or fall in love. Danger makes one receptive to romance. Danger is an aphrodisiac. To test this, researchers asked single men to cross a suspension bridge. The bridge was safe, but frightening. Some men met women on the bridge. Other men encountered the same women—but not on the bridge—in a safer setting such as a campus or an office.

The men who met the women on the trembling bridge were much more likely to ask them out on dates.

—DIANE ACKERMAN, *A Natural History of Love*

LOST...AND FOUND

ONCE I ARRIVED IN AN INDIAN TOWN EXHAUSTED after a long train ride. I found a cheap, nondescript place to stay, slept soundly for twelve hours, woke up, showered, and went exploring. Hours later, when it was time to head back, I couldn't remember the name of the hotel or where it was!

After months of staying in inns named after Lakshmi, Durga, and all the Indian gods, guest houses named Rose and Daffodil and every flower in a bouquet, and hotels named to reassure the wary traveler—Honest, Friendly, Clean Hotel—I simply blanked out.

That experience led to a simple new routine: each time I sign in at a new hotel, I take their business card and slip it into my pocket. It comes in handy when I ask for directions, especially if the name is written in more than one language. And, if I like the place, I tuck the card into my journal or pack to recommend to someone else.

—THALIA ZEPATOS, *A Journey of One's Own*

OUT THERE IN BORNEO

*O*NE OF MY TRAVEL FANTASIES has always been to go someplace so remote that I'd be transported to another reality, the one that flourished on earth before the evolution of human technocrats. The only person I know to have done that is Eric Hansen, who spent seven months in Borneo traveling in the rain forest as the natives do—setting up temporary shelters, hunting and gathering food, adapting to the rhythms of the jungle as well as the villages and longhouses.

When Hansen finally reached a logging camp near the east coast, he was ushered into the bathroom of a missionary pilot and confronted by "a brand-new bar of Dove soap, a white porcelain washbasin, and a blue terrycloth handtowel with matching washcloth." His response was an almost uncontrollable urge to leap out of the window.

"The ultimate trip," I wrote in my journal that night—our third on the Boh—"would be to get that far out; far enough out there to be scared by a bar of soap."

—TRACY JOHNSTON, *Shooting the Boh*

June 13

AN AFRICAN DESERT RAINSTORM

*W*E CAME TO THE SAHARA LATE IN THE AFTERNOON, during the descent from the mountains, as if we had passed through a transparent wall. The rain suddenly stopped, the air warmed, and a strong sun dissolved the clouds. We crested a rise, and the Sahara appeared below—a brilliant and treeless plain stretching south in naked folds to the horizon. A trace of smoke marked some unseen oasis. The view was so wide you could imagine the curvature of the earth.

The road led down into it, and the uniform plain became a rolling desert of yellow sand and ochre dirt, strewn with stone, and cut sharply by gullies. Spiny bushes had rooted along the gullies, and in the shelter of rocks. A camel grazed on thin and fragile grasses. The bus grew hot. I opened a window to let in the wind. The air smelled of baked soil, and tasted of sand. In the distance, a cluster of date palms survived untended. The sky was close, fierce, relentless. It pushed away even the memory of rain.

—WILLIAM LANGEWIESCHE, *Sahara Unveiled*

CYPRUS

*C*YPRUS REMAINED IN MY MIND...MUCH AS HEAVEN does in the minds of respectable people, as a place I should go to, though I made no preparations for getting there.

—W. H. MALLOCK, *In an Enchanted Island* (1889)

June 15

A FREE RIDE

*O*UR RIDE HOMEWARD WAS PLEASANT, NOT ONLY because of the mountain scenery but also on account of the mere pleasure of the ride…. I think that letting a ballot slip through my fingers into the ballot box—that ungraceful, unwomanly act that is to convert us at some future day into masculine beings—I think that even that will not make me feel more free, more unfettered, in plain language, more man-like than I did while galloping on my great black charger.

—ISABELLA BIRD,
A Lady's Life in the Rocky Mountains (1881)

RIVERS

*T*HOUGH THE NAMES ARE STILL MAGIC—AMAZON, Nile, Congo, Mississippi, Niger, Platte, Volga, Tiber, Seine, Ganges, Mekong, Rhine, Rhone, Colorado, Euphrates, Marne, Orinoco, Rio Grande—the rivers themselves have almost disappeared from consciousness in the modern world. Insofar as they exist in our imaginations, that existence is nostalgic.

Our railroads followed the contours of the rivers and then our highways followed the contours of the rail lines. Traveling, we move as a river moves, at two removes. Rivers and the river gods that defined our civilizations have become the sublimated symbols of everything we have done to the planet in the past 200 years. And the rivers themselves have come to function as trace memories of what we have repressed in the name of our technological mastery. They are the ecological unconscious.

—ROBERT HASS, INTRODUCTION, *The Gift of Rivers*

MOUNTAIN OF MOUNTAINS

*I*T IS HARD TO DO JUSTICE to the magnitude of the Himalayas and the height of its crowning peak. Perhaps some idea of immensity, the magnetic power, of the Himalayan mountain mass may be gathered from the fact that the liquid in a spirit-level is attracted towards it to an appreciable extent. Indeed, it exerts a force similar to the moon's on the waters of the vast Indian Ocean. And this greatest of mountain ranges rises almost abruptly from the plain of India! As for the altitude of its undisputed monarch, Everest, imagine the pinnacle of a Matterhorn on the shoulders of Mont Blanc, or Mt. Rainier, the second highest peak of the United States, capped by the very highest, Mt. Whitney. Only from the elevation of nearly five tiers of Mt. Washingtons, might one gaze down on the summit of Everest.

—COLONEL P.T. ETHERTON, ET AL,
First Over Everest! (1933)

MOUNT PARNASSUS IN GREECE

I REACHED THE TOP OF PARNASSUS: FOR HALF AN hour I saw the whole of Greece below me, a vision of incredible beauty, all its rusty headlands and misty seas and Olympus (which they call Olybus because mp = b) in the far north and *everything,* in fact, somewhere in sight: and crocus and scylla, incredibly blue ones, on the edge of the snow. When we came off the top, my guide wrapped me in a blanket and I fell asleep and woke after an hour with an icy wind and have been suffering from a miserable cough ever since: but one must be prepared to sacrifice something for trespassing on the Gods.

—FREYA STARK, LETTER (1938)

RETURN TO RAPTURE

MORE OFTEN THAN NOT, GOING back to a place where you've had a special experience is disappointing. With that in mind, I returned with my family to Kona …and yet, despite my wariness, the rapture began again. Was it the octopus we saw while snorkeling, the grass skirt one of my daughters wove under the tutelage of a sweet craft director, the dinner we ate after waiting for the local manta ray to show up, the lack of telephones and television, the stroll under the stars to our grass-thatched *hale*, the wind blowing over our bed, the sincere kindness of the staff? No, I am convinced there is a dimensional portal here, that when you are in Kona, you are not on earth at all.

How else can I explain that four days lasted three months?

—JAMES O'REILLY, "KONA DREAMTIME,"
Travelers' Tales Hawai'i

TRAIN TRAVEL

*T*RAIN TRAVEL FOR ME IS THE FICTIVE MODE. TRAINS are the stuff of stories, inside and out. From windows I have seen lovers embrace, workers pause from their travail. Women gaze longingly at the passing train; men stare with thwarted dreams in their eyes. Escapist children try to leap aboard. Narratives, like frames of film, pass by.

On the inside I have had encounters as well. I've met people who have become briefly, for the length of the ride, a lover or friend. A strange and sudden intimacy seems possible here. On the Puno-Cuzco Express through the Urubama Valley of Peru, I met a man I thought I would follow across the Andes. On the night train from Chung-king a woman stayed up half the night telling me the story of her life. On an Italian train I  met a woman who pleaded with me to go to Bulgaria with her, saying she knew it was where I needed to be. I've been invited off trains into homes, into beds, asked to walk into people's lives, all I am sure because people know a train traveler will never leave the train.

—MARY MORRIS, *Wall to Wall*

June 21

TANABATA, THE SUMMER FESTIVAL

"THIS IS IT," I SAY ALOUD. THE DRUMBEATS STARTED in the distance curving their rhythm through the puzzling streets, up to me in my five-tatami-mat apartment. The excitement and tension grew in me over the months since first hearing about Tanabata—the Summer Festival.

I jump up and run to the door, sliding on my sandals as I stumble out into the street. I press my way through the hot and humid air toward the maze of music. I reach the main street, where my blonde hair becomes lost in a sea of black locks.

Once surrounded by Japanese natives, I am struck by the kimono shuffle—the wooden sandal flip-flop click-clock. Flashes of gold, red, green, and yellow fireworks amaze my foreign eyes. Flags flap around me and seem to be suspended mid-wave by the muggy air. My soul is filled with this streaming celebration.

Easing my way through and around the crowd, I peer over toward the radiating drumbeat. Half-naked men dressed in diapers pound their thin muscled arms with fervor. Mothers, fathers, and children are drenched with sweat as the summer sun sets. Asahi beer flows cold, barbeque octopus legs dangle on sticks, and me in the land where every season is welcomed with complete exhilaration and joy.

Summer is here.

—KARA THACKER, "RHYTHMS OF JAPAN"

SCOTLAND'S BRILLIANT SCENERY

I FELL IN LOVE FOR THE FIRST TIME IN EDINBURGII, just as the British pound was about to crash. Because of interest rates and exchange rates and memories of war, the state of a nascent European Union was becoming something less than perfect. Fingers pointed toward the banks of a newly unified Germany, and because my lover was from Hamburg, we hit the road for the Highlands to spare him exposure to anger that might be looking for a target.

Heading north, we made our way up Scotland's torso toward Thurso via Inverness. Sometime before sundown and somewhere before Wick, we found ourselves near the sea on a one-lane drag decorated by sheep. We soon stopped for the night, and after a warm bed and a hot breakfast, pushed on to Dunnet Head, the northernmost point of the British mainland. We continued west, passing through Thurso and the tip of Tongue; then following the coastline, we put Cape Wrath behind us. And finally, clinging to the land's perimeter, we curved south toward the Isle of Skye.

It was here, in the midst of a warm storm wind, that the world stopped. And a moment turned. And beneath a sky divided by summer blues and somber clouds, I knew I'd seen perfection.

—KARA KNAFELC, "IN LOVE IN SCOTLAND"

June 23

LOSING (AND FINDING) ONESELF

ONCE ON A LONG TRIP DOWN A WILD RIVER, I dreamed about my city and my home every night, and upon my return, I began to dream about the river over and over again. Here, most often, is nothing more than the best perspective from which to contemplate there: one climbs the mountain to see the valley. Traveling, I had found in the course of a year of far-reaching excursions, shifted one's memory and imagination as well as one's body. The new and unknown places called forth strange, oft-forgotten correspondences and desires in the mind, so that the motion of travel takes place as much in the psyche as anywhere else. Travel offers the opportunity to find out who else one is, in that collapse of identity into geography I want to trace.

—REBECCA SOLNIT, *A Book of Migrations*

ITALY

I CAN NEVER MAKE A POEM ABOUT ITALY. ABOUT ITALY you do, you address, bless, and say adieu. Adieu Italy, beautiful Italy adieu.

—GERTRUDE STEIN, *Geography and Plays*

THE AMBIENCE OF AIRPORTS

*A*IRPORTS ARE AMONG THE ONLY SITES IN PUBLIC life where emotions are hugely sanctioned. We see people weep, shout, kiss in airports; we see them at the furthest edges of excitement and exhaustion. Airports are privileged spaces where we can see the primal states—fear, recognition, hope—writ large. But there are some of us, perhaps, sitting at the departure gate, boarding passes in hand, watching the destinations ticking over, who feel neither the pain of separation nor the exultation of wonder; who alight with the same emotions with which we embarked; who go down to the baggage carousel and watch our lives circling, circling, circling, waiting to be claimed.

—PICO IYER,
"THE SOUL OF AN INTERCONTINENTAL WANDERER"

KJOSTIND, NORWAY

*W*E WERE SINGULARLY FAVORED BY THE WEATHER, and sat a long time on the summit, while Imboden devised safe and speedy routes up the scores of magnificent peaks which surrounded us. Here, a rocky needle reminded us of the Aiguille du Dru. There, a great rock-ribbed mountain, plastered with glacier, seemed another Barre des Ecrins. To the south, the huge snowy mass of the Yoeggevarre resembled Mont Blanc. But another feature was present, never seen in Alpine views. The Lake of Thun looks exquisitely lovely at early morning from the Jungfrau. But no lake can match the heavenly blue of the fjords as they stretch mile after mile, away amidst snow-crowned mountains, away to the distant, island-gemmed Arctic Ocean. Such a view as I saw from the Kjostind my eyes had never rested on before; it alone was worth a longer journey than I had made from England.

—MRS. AUBREY LE BLOND,
Mountaineering in the Land of the Midnight Sun (1908)

June 27

CROSS-CULTURAL DIFFERENCES

WHEN I WAS LIVING IN SOUTH KOREA, A FRIEND who had traveled and lived abroad wrote to me about cross-cultural experience. She said when she first went to a place, any place, she was astounded at how radically different things were from the States. Then, the longer she stayed, the more similarities she found. The only exception she noted was Canada. When an American first goes there, she feels right at home. Then, she noted, "Everything just gets weirder and weirder."

—RICHARD TERRILL, *Saturday Night in Baoding*

A SALUTE TO REMEMBER

*I*T WAS MY LAST NIGHT ON SAFARI AND I WAS SAD TO be saying farewell. We were staying at a lovely English colonial hotel, the Nugulia Lodge at Tsavo National Park in East Africa. After dinner, I walked out on the terrace to see if there were any animals that had come to the salt lick yet that evening. There was one elephant licking the salt. I stood watching her and wondering how long her ancestors had walked these dry plains where man was born. I wondered if there would be room on the planet for her species in the next century. Suddenly, she looked up, ears waving like antennas, and glanced in my direction. Slowly she began to saunter towards the terrace. The terrace was approximately two stories high and when she stood directly in front of me, we were looking at each other eye-to-eye. I heard other people moving backwards and whispering anxiously. Someone tugged at my arm, trying to make me move away. I stood my ground and continued looking into her small, wise eyes, feeling a primal sense of awe, respect, and love for this enormous creature. After a few minutes, she raised her trunk up in the air and saluted me. I raised my arm in salute to her and Africa. Slowly and gracefully, she backed up and turned around and disappeared into the dark. I have never forgotten her.

—PAMELA CONLEY, "ON SAFARI"

A BALINESE ODYSSEY

*A*LMOST EVERY DAY OF THE YEAR IS CELEBRATED with a ceremony or ritual. One night I was awakened by a dreadful squealing noise. The next morning I discovered the neighbors had sacrificed a pig outside my window in some sort of pork chop offering to the gods ceremony. Not a day went by when I didn't see a procession of colorfully dressed women balancing pyramids of tropical fruit, cake, and flowers on their heads as offerings to the fertility goddess, or whoever the deity of the day happened to be.

—LAURIE GOUGH, *Kite Strings of the Southern Cross*

LINGERING IN BRAZIL

*H*OSPITALITY IS THE GREATEST DELAY IN BRAZILIAN travel. It is the old style of Colonial greeting; you may do what you like, you may stay for a month, but not for a day.

—SIR RICHARD BURTON,
Explorations of the Highlands of Brazil (1869)

July 1

THE FIG SELLER OF SANTIAGO

IN THE OUTDOOR MARKET OF SANTIAGO DE Compostela, baskets of figs gleam in the sun. They are purple-green. I haven't seen fresh figs for years.

"How much?" I ask in Spanish.

The fruit seller's eyes crinkle, peering at me. She ignores my question. "You don't speak Gallego?"

"No," I say. "I'm sorry."

"I'm sorry too," she says, shaking gray-streaked curls. Then, as if regretting her remark: "But your Spanish is good."

"The figs?" I repeat. "How much are they?"

"It depends," she says. "Where are you from?"

I have heard that Galicians don't give straight answers—they like to play you a bit. I tell her I'm from Boston. "And where are you from?" I ask.

"Right here," she says, with a little stamp of her foot. "Santiago."

"And how much are your figs?" I try again.

"It depends how many are bought."

"Say, a quarter kilo?"

"That would be *setenta pesetas*." About fifty cents. I pull out the coins.

She drops the figs into a plastic bag, weighs out a quarter kilo, adds a few more. I turn to go and she calls after me, "Very good Spanish!"

—LUCY McCAULEY, "WHILE IN SPAIN"

WAIKIKI, HAWAI'I

*I*T WAS A PERFECT HOUR FOR A SWIM. THE SUN WAS low in the sky and had lost its fierce daytime heat, but the sea was warm and the air balmy. I swam vigorously for about a hundred yards in the general direction of Australia, then floated on my back and gazed up at the overarching sky. Long shreds of mauve-tinted cloud, edged with gold, streamed like banners from the west. A jet droned overhead, but could not disturb the peace and beauty of the evening. The hum of the city seemed muted and distant. I emptied my mind and let the waves rock me as if I were a piece of flotsam. Occasionally, a bigger wave surged past, swamping me or lifting me in the air like a matchstick, leaving me spluttering in its wake, laughing like a boy.

I decided I would do this more often.

—DAVID LODGE, *Paradise News*

July 3

CHARTING HER OWN COURSE

I AM DEVELOPING A HIGH OPINION OF MYSELF AS A
traveler. I consider that I excel most masculine travelers, for I
travel in all countries without arms to protect me, without
Baedecker and Bradshaw to inform me, and without book companion or tobacco to console me.

—LILIAN LELAND, *Travelling Alone* (1890)

FROM SEA TO SHINING SEA

*T*HEN HOW, FINALLY, SHOULD WE CHARACTERIZE this country that continues to engage, enrage, confound, and inspire the rest of the world—even as it ceaselessly draws visitors to its shores and sends the rest of us bouncing around its borders?

I think all we can say is that it's vast, copious, and contradictory.

From Many. One.

"Always have a guide in the U.S.," writes Englishman Adam Nicolson, "it's a much more foreign place than you think."

Good advice—as far as it goes. These fifty states and assorted possessions (How easily we forget our imperial grasp of Puerto Rico, the Virgin Islands, American Samoa, Guam) comprise one of the grandest, strangest, most influential societies ever to stake out borders on planet Earth. Yet even those of us who have always lived here may benefit from the eyes and insights of plucky travelers—be they peregrinating foreigner or uprooted resident. In truth, we need regularly to be reminded about the kind of daft and beguiling land we inhabit.

—FRED SETTERBERG, *Travelers' Tales America*

July 5

SLEEPING WITH CROCODILES

*L*ATER WE WENT TO SEE THE BEAST BOB HAD BEEN shown, and there to my horror I noticed that it lay exactly three yards from where I had spent half an hour that afternoon barefooted, swimming and working on my fan-belt. Everything now clicked into place. My "fish" was beyond doubt the belly of a crocodile diving to get out of my way. Michael began stammering about the hours we had spent bathing or just soaking at the water's edge, not to mention our sleeping on beaches. "If you sleep on or near a beach," an expert on reptiles later explained, "you should always plant stakes and join them with rope to which you attach tin cans to scare the crocodiles away," adding horrified, "Where did you think they lived?" Yet this friend was no coward, for he himself had collected reptiles in Nepal. "You were," he concluded, "both lucky and mad."

—MICHEL PEISSEL, *The Great Himalayan Passage*

AGE-OLD TRAVEL WISDOM

*I*F YOU WILL HAVE A YOUNG MAN PUT HIS TRAVEL INTO a little room, and in short to gather much, this you must do. First, as was said, he must have some entrance into the language before he goeth. Then he must have such a servant or tutor as knoweth the country, as was likewise said. Let him carry with him also some card or book describing the country where he travelleth; which will be a good key to his inquiry. Let him keep also a diary. Let him not stay long in one city or town; more or less as the place deserveth, but not long; nay, when he stayeth in one city or town, let him change his lodging from one end and part of the town to another; which is great adamant of acquaintance. Let him sequester himself from the company of his countrymen, and diet in such places where there is good company of the nation where he travelleth. Let him upon his removes from one place to another, procure recommendation to some person of quality residing in the place whither he removeth; that he may use his favour in those things he desireth to see or know. Thus he may abridge his travel with much profit. As for the acquaintance which is to be sought in travel; that which is most of all profitable, is acquaintance with the secretaries and employed men of ambassadors: for so in traveling in one country he shall suck the experience of many.

—SIR FRANCIS BACON, "OF TRAVEL" (1625)

July 7

A SMALL MISUNDERSTANDING

*N*OT ONLY WAS THERE A BAD CONNECTION BUT the Irish pay phones matter of factly take your money up front. During my expensive and tolling call to a female friend back in Galway, I managed to tell her that I was coming back to Galway soon, but I couldn't get a ride in Mayo. As the phone crackled with static, I spoke louder; "I can't get a ride in Mayo!" The damn phone went dead and I vigorously cursed the telecommunications in Ireland. That was until I was informed what "getting a ride" in Ireland meant. It did take some explaining to my female friend, but it ended up, as most things do in Ireland, with a laugh.

—TIMOTHY K. EGAN, "MY ISLAND, MY ISLAND…,"
Travelers' Tales Ireland

RIO DE JANEIRO, BRAZIL

FOLLOWING A PATHWAY, I ENTERED A NOBLE FOREST, and from a height of five or six hundred feet, one of those splendid views was presented, which are so common on this side of Rio. At this elevation, the landscape attains its most brilliant tint; and every form, every shade, so completely surpasses in magnificence all that the European has ever beheld in his own country, that he knows not how to express his feelings. The general effect frequently recalled to my mind the gayest scenery of the Opera House or the great theatres.

—CHARLES DARWIN, *Journal During the Voyage of H.M.S. Beagle* (1832–36)

July 9

My Own Fireworks

*W*E'D BEEN TRAVELING FOR HOURS IN FITS AND starts, lurching from station to station, stopping in the middle of nowhere for no apparent reason. The steam locomotive spewed ash and bits of coal, which blew through the window on the wind, soiling the seats, our clothing, our bodies. As darkness fell I saw sparks flying with the grit, something I'd never noticed on these ancient Indian trains. At night the smoke was alive with fire, whole constellations of stars riding off on the breeze.

A short while later we stopped again, the locomotive shut down, the smoke and ash cleared, but the sparks continued, and as I leaned out into the sticky heat, I realized they weren't sparks at all, but the air was thick with fireflies.

—LARRY HABEGGER, "TO THE SOUTH,"
Travelers' Tales India

THE STAMP OF WILDERNESS

*T*HE SERENGETI PLAINS SPREAD FROM LAKE NYARAZA, in Tanganyika, northward beyond the lower boundaries of Kenya Colony. They are the great sanctuary of the Masai People and they harbour more wild game than any similar territory in all of East Africa. In the season of drought they are as dry and tawny as the coats of the lion that prowl them, and during the rains they provide the benison of soft grass to all the animals in a child's picture book.

They are endless and they are empty, but they are as warm with life as the waters of a tropic sea. They are webbed with the paths of eland and wildebeest and Thompson's gazelle and their hollows and valleys are trampled by thousands of zebra. I have seen a herd of buffalo invade the pastures under the occasional thorn tree groves and, now and then, the whimsically fashioned figure of a plodding rhino has moved along the horizon like a grey boulder come to life and adventure bound. There are no roads. There are no villages, no towns, no telegraph. There is nothing, as far as you can see, or walk, or ride, except grass and rocks and a few trees and the animals that live there.

—BERYL MARKHAM, *West with the Night*

July 11

WHAT DO YOU FEAR?

I'M OFTEN ASKED WHAT I'M MOST AFRAID OF WHEN I travel to Third World countries. People expect to hear something like: catching the Ebola virus, being detained by the secret police, getting mugged in a dark alley, or catching the Ebola virus from the secret police in a dark alley. Now, I don't want to marginalize the image of any of these dramatic foreign tribulations, but they generally don't worry me. I mean, as tribulations go, they're right there at the top of the list. But riding a Third World bus has got to be one of the most dangerous (and thrilling) rides on earth.

—DOUG LANSKY,
"THE ART OF RIDING A THIRD WORLD BUS,"
There's No Toilet Paper on the Road Less Traveled

EGYPT AT SUNSET

*T*HAT THE SUNSET IN EGYPT IS GORGEOUS, everybody knows; but I, for one, was not aware that there is a renewal of beauty, some time after the sun has departed and left all grey. This discharge of colour is here much what it is among the Alps, where the flame-coloured peaks become grey and ghastly as the last sunbeam leaves them. But here, everything begins to brighten again in twenty minutes; —the hills are again purple or golden, —the sands orange, —the palms verdant, —the moonlight on the water, a pale green ripple on a lilac surface: and this after-glow continues for ten minutes, when it slowly fades away.

—HARRIET MARTINEAU,
Eastern Life, Past and Present (1848)

July 13

THE ENGLISH CHANNEL

*I*T IS THE MOST MARVELOUS SEA IN THE WORLD, THE most suited for these little adventures; it is crammed with strange towns, differing one from the other; it has two opposite peoples upon either side, and hills, and varying climates, and the hundred shapes and colors of the earth, here rocks, there sand, there cliffs, and there marshy shores. It is a little world. And what is more, it is a kind of inland sea.

—HILAIRE BELLOC, *Hills and the Sea* (1906)

THE PERFECTION OF FRANCE

*W*E HAVE COME FIVE HUNDRED MILES BY RAIL through the heart of France. What a bewitching land it is!—What a garden! Surely the leagues of bright green lawns are swept and brushed and watered every day, and their grasses trimmed by the barber. Surely the hedges are shaped and measured, and their symmetry preserved, by the most architectural of gardeners. Surely the long straight rows of stately poplars that divide the beautiful landscape like the squares of a chequer-board are set with line and plummet, and their uniform height determined with a spirit-level. Surely the straight, smooth, pure white turnpikes are jackplaned and sandpapered  every day. How else are these marvels of symmetry, cleanliness, and order attained? It is wonderful. There are no unsightly stone walls, and never a fence of any kind. There is no dirt, no decay, no rubbish anywhere—nothing that even hints at untidiness—nothing that ever suggests neglect. All is orderly and beautiful—everything is charming to the eye.

—MARK TWAIN, *The Innocents Abroad* (1869)

July 15

A FUTILE TEACHING IN NEPAL

*I*T WAS OUR WINTER HOLIDAY AND WE WERE VISITING A relative in the *tarai*. Since we were city boys, naturally we wanted to go hunting. Our cousin was a *zamindar* and he indicated that hunting to him was as natural as breathing. So, no problem, he'd take us city kids to hunt in the jungle, which was his backyard.

We woke up at four in the morning; it was very cold and pitch black. A bullock cart waited for us. Our cousin, with his double-barreled gun, my brother, and I got into the cart. The driver tapped the bulls and we were off. A *shikari* walked along the cart, holding a kerosene lamp that illuminated the rutted path in the forest.

After what seemed like a very long time, the cart halted. Silence. I heard the *shikari* whisper, "To your left, sir."

Our cousin got up and aimed. I looked in the direction of the pointed gun and there, in the feeble light of the misty dawn, I saw half a dozen deer of various sizes grazing in the clearing. They were astonishingly beautiful and delicate—and I suddenly regretted my city boy's glamorous fantasies of going hunting.

A loud bang! and the deer scattered. Not one fell. A second bang! but the deer had disappeared. And just as our cousin disappointedly lowered his gun, a deer re-appeared into the clearing, looked around, and gracefully bounded away.

I have never gone hunting since.

—RAJENDRA S. KHADKA, *Travelers' Tales Nepal*

UNDER THE VEILS OF CASABLANCA

YOUNG WOMEN IN PINK LAB COATS GREETED ME AT THE baths, and I paid about $18 for "everything." In the steam room women were sitting on stools in front of marble cisterns, pouring basins of water over their heads, rubbing themselves with black soap. They chatted and touched each other, nonchalantly lifting up a breast to wash underneath, or spreading their legs to soap their inner thighs. It was unlike the little bubble of privacy—and body shame—that surrounds women in western baths.

In the outer room, a beefy woman took my scratchy mitt from me and scrubbed my whole body pink and nearly raw. As I rinsed off and recuperated, I realized my skin felt incredibly soft and clean. The attendant led me to another room, where a masseuse gave me a wonderful massage with oil.

Rinsed, I was directed to the relaxation room. The other women had the intensity of relaxation that only comes when someone has to go back to the constant demands of a husband and children. This was their sanctum. They seemed so casual in their pajamas, tiger-print leggings, and sparkly t-shirts, that I didn't think they were the ones I'd seen on the streets, veiled head-to-toe. But one by one they wrapped their hair in a towel and tossed on a *djellaba*. They walked out of the baths, anonymous. In my dress and light hair, I was once again exposed. I wished, for a moment, for a *djellaba* of my own.

—LAURA FRASER, "AT THE BATHS"

BRING HOME THE WORLD

*A*LL TRAVEL HAS ITS ADVANTAGES. IF THE PASSENGER visits better countries, he may learn to improve his own, and if fortune carries him to worse, he may learn to enjoy it.

—SAMUEL JOHNSON (1709–1784)

THE DANCE OF LOVE

*A*NDALUCÍA AWAKENS AT THE SOUND OF TAPPING. The wooden stage welcomes Antonio and Lola for *sevillanas*. The guitarists lower their heads to better hear the sounds of their *pizzicato* and to allow the dancers a private moment to prepare their souls for the most passionate dance. Soon Antonia and Lola begin to move through the four parts, the *coplas*, that are the *sevillana*.

The Acquaintance: Facing each other, Lola shows the swirl of her skirt and her ability to perform. Antonio flirts through his strong and clear tapping. Shy crossings end with a salute to the audience.

The Awakening of Love: The dancers' crossings become much quicker and more passionate, with Antonio leading very close turns, their faces two inches apart.

The Social Presentation: The dancing becomes cold for a few seconds, the dancers/lovers honoring the memory of their precious independence from each other. Now they begin the most difficult tapping; turning to face the audience and presenting themselves as a couple.

The Promise of Eternal Love: This is the dance of the consumed love. Antonio kneels in the eight crossings, and there is a clamourous applause from the many visitors at the *taverna* tonight.

—CRISTINA DEL SOL, *"Sueños," Travelers' Tales Spain*

A SIMPLE TOUCH

I DON'T KNOW WHAT IRELAND DOES TO A PERSON—
rushes in, stakes a claim. It is an infusion that breathes salty
fresh air, stinging breezes, a crinkled smile from that old man
down the bar. Is it the fire that each person breathes as they open
their mouths to speak or sing? Maybe it is the simplicity of life,
the stone walls of the countryside, the hungry look of those who
want to be anywhere but there. The frank open eyes that ask me
for the basic fulfillment of a touch. A simple touch.

—MIREYA MORALES QUIRIE,
"IRISH MEMORIES"

ISLANDS

*H*OW WONDERFUL ARE ISLANDS! THE PAST AND the future are cut off; only the present remains. Existence in the present gives island living an extra vividness and purity. One lives like a child or a saint in the immediacy of the here and now. Every day, every act, is an island, washed by time and space, and has an island's completion. People too become like islands in such an atmosphere, self-contained, whole and serene; respecting other people's solitude, not intruding on their shores, standing back in reverence before the miracle of each other individual.

—ANNE MORROW LINDBERGH, *Gift from the Sea*

July 21

AN ARAB DINNER

*A*RABS IGNORE THE DELIGHTFUL FRENCH ART OF prolonging a dinner. After washing your hands, you sit down, throw an embroidered napkin over your knees, and with a *"Bismillah,"* by way of grace, plunge your hand into the attractive dish, changing *ad libitum*, occasionally sucking your fingertips as boys do lollipops, and varying that diversion by cramming a chosen morsel into a friend's mouth. When your hunger is satisfied, you do not sit for your companions; you exclaim *"Al Hamd!"* edge away from the tray, wash your hands and mouth with soap, display signs of repletion, otherwise you will be pressed to eat more, seize your pipe, sip your coffee, and take your *"Kayf."* Nor is it customary, in these lands, to sit together after dinner—the evening prayer cuts short the séance.

—SIR RICHARD BURTON, *Personal Narrative of a Pilgrimage
to Al-Madinah and Meccah* (1855–56)

REMNANTS OF ROME

*O*NE LOSES SIGHT OF ALL DABBLING AND PRETENSION when seated at the feet of dead Rome—Rome so grand and beautiful upon her bier. Art is dead here; the few sparkles that sometimes break through the embers cannot make a flame; but the relics of the past are great enough, over-great; we should do nothing but sit, and weep, and worship.

MARGARET FULLER OSSOLI, *At Home and Abroad* (1848)

The Sweet Skim of the Sea

 *A*ND SO WE STEAM OUT. AND ALMOST at once the ship begins to take a long, slow, dizzy dip, and a fainting swoon upwards, and a long, slow, dizzy dip, slipping away from beneath one. The q-b turns pale. Up comes the deck in that fainting swoon backwards—then down it fades in that indescribable slither forwards. It is all quite gentle—quite, quite gentle. But oh, so long, and so slow, and so dizzy.

"Rather pleasant!" say I to the q-b.

"Yes. Rather lovely really!" she answers wistfully. To tell the truth there is something in the long, slow lift of the ship, and her long, slow slide forwards which makes my heart beat with joy. It is the motion of freedom. To feel her come up—then slide slowly forward, with the magic gallop of elemental space. That long, slow, wavering rhythmic rise and fall of the ship, with waters snorting as it were from her nostrils, oh, God, what a joy it is to the wild innermost soul. One is free at last—and lilting in a slow flight of the elements, winging outwards.

—D. H. LAWRENCE, *Sea and Sardinia* (1921)

OPEN YOURSELF UP TO TRAVEL

*I*F YOU HAVE BEEN REARED IN THE BELIEF THAT YOUR own country, or your own state, town, or hamlet, contains all that is good in the world, whether of moral excellence, mental development, or mechanical skill, you must prepare to eradicate that belief at an early date.

To an observant and thoughtful individual the invariable effect of travel is to teach respect for the opinions, the faith, or the ways of others, and to convince him that other civilizations than his own are worthy of consideration.

—THOMAS W. KNOX, *How to Travel* (1881)

July 25

BRUSSELS, BELGIUM

IF ANY PERSON WANTS TO BE HAPPY I SHOULD ADVISE the Parc. You sit drinking iced drinks and smoking penny cigars under great old trees. The band place, covered walks, etc., are all lit up. And you can't fancy how beautiful was the contrast of the great masses of lamp-lit foliage and the dark sapphire night sky, with just one blue star set overhead in the middle of the largest patch. In the dark walks, too, there are crowds of people whose faces you cannot see, and here and there a colossal white statue at the corner of an alley that gives the place a nice *artificial*, eighteenth-century sentiment. There was a good deal of summer lightning blinking overhead, and the black avenues and white statues leap out every minute into short-lived distinctness.

—ROBERT LOUIS STEVENSON,
LETTER TO HIS MOTHER (1872)

CURITIBA, BRAZIL

*A*T THE FAR END OF THE WOODEN BRIDGE IS A SMALL lake in an old granite quarry. Two white swans glide across the still water, their long necks curling into feathered question marks.

As the morning sun crests the treetops, I am startled to hear the rumblings of Bach's Toccata and Fugue coming from loudspeakers attached to the soaring stone walls. I sit watching the play of light on the lake, listening to the deep drone until it slowly fades into the languorous strains of the Brandenburg Concertos, and the sheer blue sky hosts the hypnotic sounds of joyously conversing violins.

Abruptly the spell is split by the shrill cries of a chainsaw at the edge of the park. Metal teeth gnash the air. The forest moans as great branches crash to the ground. An unseen hand turns up the volume of the music, producing a strange syncopation of falling trees and soaring violins.

A dusty trunk in the attic of my memory opens and I recall the legend about Bach. One brutal winter, a frost destroyed all the apple trees in the composer's grove, but one. Desperate to save his last tree, Bach ventured out to offer it the only protection he could think of—the manuscript of the Brandenburgs. With those parchment bandages, he tenderly wrapped the bark of the dying tree.

In the brief interlude, the swans are utterly still. Hearing nothing, they glide on, moved from below, by the unseen. They cross the canyon lake again and again, poised for the next waves of sound.

—PHIL COUSINEAU, "BACH IN BRAZIL"

July 27

THE GULF STREAM

*T*HE BIGGEST REASON YOU LIVE IN CUBA IS THE great, deep blue river, three-quarters of a mile to a mile deep and sixty to eighty miles across, that you can reach in thirty minutes from the door of your farmhouse, riding through beautiful country to get to it, that has, when the river is right, the finest fishing I have ever known.

When the Gulf Stream is running well, it is a dark blue and there are whirlpools along the edges.

—ERNEST HEMINGWAY, *Holiday Magazine* (1949)

WHEN WATER FALLS

*T*HE RUSH OF WATER IS A TRAVELLER'S ELIXIR! Nothing can beat one of the great waterfalls, when it comes to the exhilaration of foreign travel. At Tisisat, on the Blue Nile below Lake Tana, you may sit meditatively beneath a gourd beside the water's turmoil, lollopped about by occasional baboons, interrogated sometimes by courteous tribesmen, and feeling like one of those distant poised figures in the background of explorers' engravings. At Tequendama in Colombia, on the other hand, you may feel yourself physically shaken by the force of the water—more an eruption than a fall, as though some hidden giant has been blocking the Rio Bogota with his thumb, like a boy with a bath tap. And undiminished, remains the marvel of those tremendous cousins of the spectacular, Niagara and Victoria, the touch of whose spray upon one's cheek can still give the most blasé wanderer a sense of complacency.

—JAN MORRIS, *Travels*

July 29

DESERT CONVENTIONS

"*W*HAT IS 'THE NEWS'?" IT IS THE QUESTION which follows every encounter in the desert, even between strangers. Given a chance the Bedu will gossip for hours, as they had done last night, and nothing is too trivial for them to recount. There is no reticence in the desert. If a man distinguishes himself he knows that his fame will be widespread; if he disgraces himself he knows that the story of his shame will inevitably be heard in every encampment. It is this fear of public opinion which enforces at all times the rigid conventions of the desert. The consciousness that they are always before an audience makes many of their actions theatrical. Glubb once told me of a Bedu sheikh who was known as "The Host of the Wolfs," because whenever he heard a wolf howl round his tent he ordered his son to take a goat out to the desert, saying he would have no one call on him for dinner in vain.

—WILFRED THESIGER, *Arabian Sands*

HOME AGAIN

*H*OW CAN I DESCRIBE THE JOY THAT FILLED MY heart when the shores of my own country first greeted my eyes through the gray atmosphere of the sea, or what emotions took possession of me while sailing up the stream. I saw the grand Statue of Liberty, the great city, and thousands of flags waving in the fresh morning's breeze. No one who has not wandered away from home and friends can understand the pleasure of being once more among their own. I simply drank deep breaths of calm, sweet gladness, and gazed about me so eagerly that my "seeing machinery" was out of order and needed a rest. I was trying to see everything at once, and was in danger of having a curvature of vision, and a chance of never having a good, straight stare again.

—MRS. WILLIAM BECKMAN, *Backsheesh* (1900)

July 31

HOOK, LINE & SINKER

ONE FISH-SELLER IN THE BOQUERIA MARKET CAME to regard me as her personal property: she made it clear that I could only buy fish from her. She would lie in wait for me as I wandered from stall to stall and then pounce, demanding to know what I wanted, and insist that she had it at the best price. If I hinted that the prawns she wanted me to buy had been frozen, she would protest vociferously, calling people over to attest to the freshness of all the fish and seafood on her stall. She had me hooked.

—COLM TÓIBÍN, *Homage to Barcelona*

WHAT BETTER TIME TO GO TO PARIS?

*T*O BE IN PARIS IN AUGUST ALWAYS MAKES ME feel that I'm in the largest and most elegant village in the world. With its population depleted, it becomes more spacious and more airy. The boulevards look wider. The trees in the parks and gardens have room to breathe. And the whole rhythm of the place changes, as if the foot has been lifted from the urban accelerator. People stroll and look around, instead of barreling along the streets with their heads down, late for something. The café waiters slow down to a Mediterranean amble, and nobody minds that service is less brisk than usual. The cab drivers restrain their natural passion for sounding their horns every ten seconds, and occasionally deign to chat to their passengers. Couples picnic by the Seine and in the Tuileries. It's not unknown to see a gendarme grin. Paris is *en vacances*.

—PETER MAYLE, "OH TO BE IN PARIS"

LIFE ON A MOUNTAIN

AIMLESS WANDERING THROUGH THE MOUNTAINS remains to me a memory of unspoiled beauty. The mountain draws a man to itself, to the sky, to man. There the struggle that reigns within everything and among all things is even more marked, but purer, unsullied by daily cares and wants. It is the struggle between light and darkness. Only there on the mountain are the nights so vast, so dark, and the mornings so gleaming. There is a struggle within everything and among all things. But above it there is a heavenly peace, something harmonious and immovable. The heavens impose the question: Who are we? From whence have we come? Where do we go? Where are the beginnings in time and space? No need to feel impatience or anger over the answer, no matter what it will be. Men on the mountain are an even greater mystery. And the stars are as near and familiar as men. The earth and sky and life become unfathomable, daily riddles that arise spontaneously, and that demand an answer. And so, forever, all must give reply. All, from the old man to the child. For the mountain is not for a tale, but a poem and for contemplation, and for purified emotion and naked passion. Life on the mountain is not easier or more comfortable, but it is loftier in everything. There are no barriers between man and the sky. Only the birds and the clouds soar by.

—MILOVAN DJILAS, *Land without Justice*

THE LONDON ZOO

*W*HEN I FIND MYSELF IN A STRANGE CITY, AT A loose end, waiting as one does eternally in strange cities for a boat, a plane, or an interview—when time seems to stop and the universe seems to have dwindled to an unending series of hotel corridors, lavatories, and lounges—I tend to go to the zoo.... You can learn a great deal about the character of a country or city by going to its zoo and studying its arrangement and the behaviour of the animals. The London Zoo is an animal microcosm of London, and even the lions, as a rule, behave as if they had been born in South Kensington.

—LEONARD WOOLF, *Downhill All the Way*

August 4

CAPTIVATED BY THE DESERT

CAMELS APPEARED ON OUR LEFT HAND: FIRST A FEW here and there, then more and more till the whole herd came browsing along, five hundred or more. I got out and went among them to photograph. The two Beduin leaders, dressed gorgeously, perched high up and swinging slowly with the movement of their beasts, shouted out to me, but the Beduin Arabic is beyond me. I can't tell you what a wonderful sight it was: as if one were suddenly in the very morning of the world among the people of Abraham or Jacob. The great gentle creatures came browsing and moving and pausing, rolling gently over the landscape like a brown wave just a little browner than the desert that carried it. Their huge legs rose up all around me like columns; the foals were frisking about: the herdsmen rode here and there. I stood in a kind of ecstasy among them. It seemed as if they were not so much moving as flowing along, with something indescribably fresh and peaceful and free about it all, as if the struggle of all these thousands of years had never been, since first they started wandering. I never imagined that my first sight of the desert would come with such a shock of beauty and enslave me right away.

—FREYA STARK, *Letters from Syria* (1927–1928)

EGYPT ON FOOT

"*A*H, YES, VIEW IS VERY BEST FROM THERE. YOU can see all three pyramids in a line, you can see the Sphinx, the Nile, and all of Cairo. But no walk," he said. "Is too far. You need camel." He turned to look admiringly at his beast. It is said that the Koran contains ninety-nine names for Allah, and that the camel looks so smug because he alone knows the one hundredth.

"Do you read Arabic?" I asked the man. Some of his colleagues had not.

"Yes, of course."

I showed him the note I had, on a sudden inspiration, asked my hotel manager to write in Arabic at the back of my notebook earlier that morning: I HAVE VERY BAD HEMORRHOIDS. I CANNOT POSSIBLY SIT ON A CAMEL.

—BRAD NEWSHAM, *Take Me With You*

August 6

THE BEAUTY OF RIVERS

I LOVE RIVERS. I WAS BORN ON THE BANKS OF THE Thames and, like my father before me, I had spent a great deal of time both on it and in it. I enjoy visiting their sources: Thames Head, in a green meadow in the Cotswolds; the river Po coming out from under a heap of boulders among the debris left by picnickers by Monte Viso; the Isonzo bubbling up over clean sand in a deep cleft in the rock in the Julian Alps; the Danube (or one of its sources) emerging in baroque splendor in a palace garden at Donaueschingen. I like exploring them. I like the way in which they grow deeper and wider and dirtier but always, however dirty they become, managing to retain some of the beauty with which there were born.

—ERIC NEWBY, *Slowly Down the Ganges*

THE POWER OF MUSIC

*M*Y HUSBAND LAWRENCE'S MUSIC WAS AS BIG A hit in the north as it had been in the south. Our hosts the O'Kanes persuaded him to bring his fiddle with him one evening. They had a friend Ann who also played the fiddle. But Ann hadn't touched the fiddle in months. Her husband had died in an accident a few months before, and she was expecting a baby. She had withdrawn into her sorrow. Wise in the way of the spirit, the O'Kanes had a plan.

That night at the family's favorite watering hole, Lawrence entertained our group with waltzes and reels. He poured his heart into hornpipes and jigs. Exhausted, he finally put his instrument down. Elderly Mrs. O'Kane ordered vodka. The pub filled up with warmth and music and a hearty camaraderie. And in the midst of the chaos a marvelous thing happened. Of course the O'Kanes had expected it would. As our spirits rose and our group became louder, the gaiety in the room became such a force that not even Ann could resist it. Reaching over the table, a song most assuredly forming in her mind, she picked up Lawrence's fiddle and played.

—LINDA WATANABE MCFERRIN, "FIDDLIN' AROUND,"
Travelers' Tales Ireland

August 8

THE TRAVEL HIGH

*A*S A TRAVELER I CAN ACHIEVE A KIND OF HIGH, A somewhat altered state of consciousness. I think it must be what athletes feel. I am transported out of myself, into another dimension in time and space. While the journey is on buses and across land, I begin another journey inside my head, a journey of memory and sensation, of past merging with present, of time growing insignificant.

—MARY MORRIS, *Nothing to Declare*

STAYING IN ONE PLACE

THIS COUNTRY THROUGH WHICH I HAVE BEEN hurled for four days has become stationary at last; instead of rushing past me, it has slowed down and finally stopped; the hills stand still, they allow me to observe them; I no longer catch but a passing glimpse of them in certain light, but may watch their changes during any hour of the day; I may walk over them and see their stones lying quiet, may become acquainted with the small life of their insects and lichens; I am no longer a traveler, but an inhabitant.

—VITA SACKVILLE-WEST, *Passenger to Tehran*

FALKLAND ISLANDS

*O*NE SEEMED TO HAVE REACHED THE VERY END OF the world.... I have seen many wild islands in many stormy seas, and some of them more bare and forbidding than this, but never any inhabited spot that seemed so entirely desolate and solitary and featureless. There was nothing for the eye to dwell upon, no lake, no river, no mountain—only scattered and shapeless hills—a land without form or expression, yet with a certain simple and primitive beauty in the colours of the yellow grass and grey-blue rocks, shining through clear air, with the sea-wind singing over them.

Anyone who today desires seclusion to think out a new philosophy might find this a fitting place of peace, if only he could learn to endure the perpetual drive of the wind. The climate is extremely healthy, but the winds are so strong and incessant that everybody goes about stooping forward.

—JAMES BRYCE, *South America* (1912)

STUCK ON BOARD IN SIGHT OF SPAIN

I WAS DEPRIVED OF THE PLEASURE OF DESCRIBING THIS city, as we were not permitted to stay there. This was at first surprising to me, for I could not conceive of any cause why I should not see the people of Cadiz; and I grieved the more at it, as I had informed my female friends at Manila that I was to visit Cadiz, and therefore was under various commands from them to some of their friends in the city. We were not permitted to stay in the port when it was known that we had come from Manila many months before, and that the cholera was there; our journals, also, showed that two of our men had died of this disorder. The authorities were very peremptory on this point, and threatened to fire into us if we did not depart instantly. This was silly as it was timid and arbitrary, for after so many months, if the disease had been contagious we were free from any infection, and could not have communicated it to the people of Cadiz. When we bring matters home to us, how much better do we reason than when our remarks are general. How ridiculous were these quarantine laws to us, who had been out of danger over the distance of nearly fifteen thousand miles of ocean! Not having a single man sick of any contagious disease, nor of any other, except accidental indisposition, we were forced to leave this port without discharging a particle of cargo, and to direct our course to Bordeaux.

—ABBY JANE MORRELL, *Narrative of a Voyage* (1833)

ONE ROOM... ONE NIGHT

"NO...WE HAVE NO ROOMS AVAILABLE," THE YOUNG Chinese woman politely smiled. "But, there must be one room...for my wife and I...just for one night...won't you please check again?" Her smile drooped and she looked slightly surprised.

And we took our small pile of luggage to a nearby pair of slightly worn chairs. As we sat we watched the clerk carefully, not actually staring, but making eye contact often enough so that she couldn't pretend we had disappeared. After thirty minutes I returned to the desk. "Would you please check to see if there is one room available?" The clerk was less friendly now. Again, she came up empty handed. "That's OK. We can wait." And we did.

After a couple more attempts, a young man meticulously dressed appeared at our side. He smiled politely and introduced himself as the manager. Again I jumped in, as politely as possible. "I understand there are no rooms available now...but we are willing to wait...as long as necessary."

I think it was that last phrase that got him. Immediately a key appeared. He returned. "One room, one night?" He asked carefully.

"Yes," I assured him. He offered the key and we all smiled. It was a "win-win" smile. We got our room. They got rid of us. And when we found that room and realized that it was in a wing of the hotel that was completely empty that smile turned into an uncontrollable laugh.

—DAVID KRAVITZ, "POLITE PERSISTENCE"

TRAVEL PREPARATIONS

I TOLD HIM I INTENDED GOING TO WEST AFRICA AND
he said, "When you have made up your mind to go to West
Africa the very best thing you can do, is to get it unmade again
and go to Scotland instead; but if your intelligence is not strong
enough to do so, abstain from exposing yourself to the direct
rays of the sun, take four grains of quinine every day for a fort-
night before you reach the Rivers, and get yourself some intro-
ductions to the Wesleyans: they are the only people on the Coast
who have got a hearse with feathers.

—MARY KINGSLEY,
Travels in West Africa (1897)

August 14

TRAVEL AT ANY AGE

*T*HERE THEY WERE BY THE HUNDREDS—AMERICANS, Scandinavians, British, French, German—all over sixty, many enjoying their first Spanish holiday on the Costa del Sol, others returning a second or third time, still holding hands or linking arms affectionately after decades of marriage.

For many it was the adventure of a lifetime. They had worked hard for decades as laborers, educators, administrators, government officials, office workers, and storekeepers. They had saved their kronen, pounds, francs, deutschmarks, dollars to buy new sport clothes and to enjoy the luxurious tourist hotels along the beaches.

The greatest gathering of hand-holders came usually after siesta late in the day along the beaches and main shopping strips. Rarely do we see the gray-and-white-haired couples holding hands along the California, Florida, or Cape Cod coasts. Was there a message and a lesson to be learned, we wondered, creeping close to the geriatric era as we were?

I thought back to the comment of the handsome white-haired gentleman in plaid bathing trunks, holding his pretty wife's hand, who bounded out of a hotel elevator, beaming: "Yes it is old folks home, geriatric row here, maybe, but isn't it fun?"

—BLYTHE FOOTE FINKE, "TOUCHING IMPROVES A VACATION,"
Travelers' Tales Spain

ON THE COLORADO RIVER

*D*URING FLOODING IN THE GRAND CANYON, I stood with the reverent boatman and renegade Wesley Smith above Hance Rapids, overlooking the huge hydraulics we were faced with navigating. The water was higher than we had seen in many seasons on the river. Hance looked big and ugly, with no clear path through. Upstream, the reservoir called Lake Powell had more than filled, and Glen Canyon Dam seemed shaky to those of us living our lives downstream. Chunks of the dam's concrete had washed through the spillways. As boatmen, we felt both thrilled and terrified, not knowing whether the dam would burst and we'd be riding the Big One to the Gulf of California. Probably we'd just continue to experience the newest form of water torture, in which the river rose a lot every day but no one could predict when it would stop.

Observing the rapids at Hance, Wesley said, "We'll have to offer extra prayers to the river gods to let us through."

Although frightened of the big water, I disagreed.

"No," I said. "You just have to put your boat in the right place." Wesley turned to me with a huge grin, delighted that I presumed our fates were in our own hands.

—REBECCA LAWTON, "IMBRICATION"

August 16

GOING SOLO

*A*S THE MILES PASSED, IT BECAME A RITE OF PASSAGE, an initiation into an adulthood carved by tools of my choice. It started a process of moving toward my own future—a simultaneously fearful and fearless act. Every woman would benefit from a solitary trip like this. The fear of would-be rapists or murderers still exists for me, but it is offset by the trust I have in my own ability to defend myself.

—CHRISTINE WEEBER, "AN UNLADYLIKE JOURNEY," *Solo*

FIJI

*O*N A COLORFULLY PAINTED BUS IN FIJI, PACKED with an assortment of humanity, I first met Jamala.

"There are many people on the bus today," she announced in textbook English. She was on her way home from third grade —perky, bright, inquisitive. For the rest of our bus ride together, she peppered me with questions. Where was I from? How did I like Fiji? Was I married? Did I have any children?

I answered her questions and asked some of my own as we sucked on hard candies from my bag, sticky now from the humidity. By the time we had arrived at the bus stop where Jamala got off—to walk up the dirt road into the sugar cane fields to the house she shared with her parents and sisters—she had carefully written my address in her blue-lined notebook.

Soon after I received a small envelope, wrinkled and smudged with a message written on the back, "Fly, fly, my letter quickly, to my dear friend." It was from Jamala, full of news about her school and her family. "Come back and visit me soon," she pleaded. "We will be so happy when I can see you again."

That was six years ago and in letters back and forth, we continue to learn about each other. She is older now, in high school, but just as curious and full of spirit as that first day on the bus. I have not been back to Fiji, but one day I will return and walk up that dirt road to Jamala's house, to see my friend.

—TARA AUSTEN WEAVER, "ON THE BUS"

THE BEAUTY OF BESANÇON

*B*ESANÇON STANDS LIKE A SORT of peninsula in a horseshoe of river. You will not learn from guide-books that the very tiles on the roofs seem to be of some quainter and more delicate colour than the tiles of all the other towns of the world; that the tiles look like the little clouds of some strange sunset, or like the lustrous scales of some strange fish. They will not tell you that in this town the eye cannot rest on anything without finding it in some way attractive and even elvish, a carved face at a street corner, a gleam of green fields through a stunted arch, or some unexpected colour for the enamel of a spire or dome.

—G. K. CHESTERTON, *Tremendous Trifles* (1909)

DRIFTING

*S*OONER OR LATER, ALL VAGABONDS DISCOVER THAT something strange happens to them en route. They become aware of having wandered into a subtle network of coincidence and serendipity that eludes explanation. On tip-toes, magic enters.

—ED BURYN, *Vagabonding in the USA*

FLORENCE, ITALY

*F*LORENCE IS BEAUTIFUL, AS I HAVE SAID BEFORE, and must say again and again, most beautiful. The river rushes through the midst of its palaces like a crystal arrow, and it is hard to tell, when you see all by the clear sunset, whether those churches, and houses, and windows, and bridges, and people walking, in the water or out of the water, are the real walls and windows, and bridges, and people, and churches.

—ELIZABETH BARRETT BROWNING,
LETTER TO MR. BOYD (1847)

MOMENTS

O H, I HAVE HAD MY MOMENTS, AND IF I HAD TO DO it over again, I'd have more of them. In fact, I'd have nothing else. Just moments, one right after another. I would go places and do things and travel lighter than I have. I would start barefoot earlier in the spring and stay that way later in the fall. I would play hooky more often. I would ride more merry-go-rounds. I'd pick more daisies.

—NADINE STAIR, *If I Had My Life to Live Over Again*

August 22

PRAGUE, CZECHOSLOVAKIA

*P*RAGUE SEEMED—IT STILL SEEMS, AFTER MANY rival cities—not only one of the most beautiful places in the world, but one of the strangest. Fear, piety, zeal, strife, and pride, tempered in the end by the milder impulses of munificence and learning and *douceur de vivre*, had flung up an unusual array of grand and unenigmatic monuments. The city, however, was scattered with darker, more reticent, less easily decipherable clues. There were moments when every detail seemed the tip of a phalanx of inexplicable phantoms. This recurring and slightly sinister feeling was fortified by the conviction that Prague, of all my halts including Vienna itself, was the place which the word *Mitteleuropa*, and all that it implies, fitted most aptly. History pressed heavily upon it. Built a hundred miles north of the Danube and three hundred east of the Rhine, it seemed, somehow, out of reach; far withdrawn into the conjectural hinterland of a world the Romans never knew.

—PATRICK LEIGH FERMOR, *A Time of Gifts*

DELIGHT IN YOKOHAMA

*I*N YOKOHAMA, I WENT TO THE HUNDRED STEPS, AT the top of which lives a Japanese belle, Oyuchisan, who is the theme for artist and pet, and the admiration of tourists. One of the pleasant events of my stay was the luncheon given for me on the *Omaha*, the American war vessel lying at Yokohama. I took several drives, enjoying the novelty of having a Japanese running by the horses' heads all the while. I ate rice and eel. I visited the curio shops, one of which is built in imitation of a Japanese house, and was charmed with the exquisite art I saw therein; in short, I found nothing but what delighted the finer senses while in Japan.

—ELIZABETH COCHRANE SEAMAN, *Nellie Bly's Book* (1890)

August 24

THE BEAUTY OF RUSSIA

*W*E GAVE FIVE OR SIX HOURS TO A STROLL through this wonderful city, a city of white houses and green roofs, of conical towers that rise one out of another like a

foreshortened telescope; of bulging gilded domes, in which you see, as in a looking-glass, distorted pictures of the city; of churches which look, outside, like bunches of variegated cactus (some branches crowned with green prickly buds, others with blue, and others with red and white) and which, inside, are hung all round with *eikons* and lamps, and lined with illuminated pictures up to the very roof; and,

finally, of pavement that goes up and down like a ploughed field, and *drojky*-drivers who insist on being paid 30 percent extra today, "because it is the Empress's birthday."

—LEWIS CARROLL, *Diary* (1867)

LOCH LOMOND

*W*E HAD NOT CLIMBED FAR WHEN WE WERE stopped by a sudden burst of prospect, so singular and beautiful that it was like a flash of images from another world. We stood with our backs to the hill of the island, which we were ascending, and which shut out Ben Lomond entirely, and all the upper part of the lake, and we looked towards the foot of the lake, scattered over with islands without beginning and without end. The sun shone, and the distant hills were visible, some through sunny mists, others in gloom with patches of sunshine; the lake was lost under the low and distant hills, and the islands lost in the lake, which was all in motion with traveling fields of light, or dark shadows under rainy clouds. There are many hills, but no commanding eminence at a distance to confine the prospect, so that the land seemed endless as the water.

—DOROTHY WORDSWORTH, *Journal* (1803)

August 26

AMAZON

*W*HEN I AM ASKED WHAT THE JUNGLE WAS LIKE, those are the places I first remember—where the river narrowed to forty feet and the green walls closed off much of the sky—not the openness of the lower river or the big skies of the Rio Negro. I have tried to think of a word or a sentence to pass off as a quick explanation, but the Amazon cannot be distilled, though many try, including me.

The more I thought about it, the more I sensed the Amazon was like the tree that fell the night before and the noise it made. Maybe even the absurdity the philosophers argued about had meaning. The Amazon, and every other point in the universe, was an immense interaction, a composite of everyone's stories, and everyone who had stepped foot in it added to its form, even if a good part of it was lies. The Amazon is a tangle of life fighting for a piece of the sky, a pressure of green that forces you to react. It is a place that, with its bugs and its heat and sun and animals and size and diseases, is always at you. It never lets up until it draws you out, and when you become part of the tangle, then for you, that is the Amazon.

—PAUL ZALIS, *Who Is the River*

A GOOD BOOK

'TIS A GOOD RULE IN EVERY JOURNEY TO PROVIDE some piece of liberal study to rescue the hours which bad weather, bad company, and taverns steal from the best economist. Classics which at home are drowsily read have a strange charm in a country inn, or in the transom of a merchant brig. I remember that some of the happiest and most valuable hours I have owed to books, passed, many years ago, on shipboard. The worst impediment I have found at sea is the want of light in the cabin.

—RALPH WALDO EMERSON, *English Traits* (1856)

August 28

SACRED OFFERINGS IN LADAKH

*W*E PROCEEDED EASTWARD ALONG THE VALLEY, OUR
little horses picking their way among the stones, and
camped each evening beside another rushing stream. We rode
from monastery to monastery. Lamas in dark red robes greeted
us quietly and led us through smoky, richly frescoed rooms,
pungent with incense and hung with elaborate tapestries. We
passed beneath the gilded eyes of inscrutable gods.

Our Ladakhi guide, Wangchok, patiently revealed the lessons of the paintings and statues. "Compassion is the best quality," he said. "Buddhism teaches be kind, be polite, be cheerful,
always tell the truth. But best is to have compassion for all things
living." And the worst? "Egotism, individualism, materialism.
Jealousy, ignorance, greed."

We Americans exchanged uneasy glances. Often we saw
lamas offering to the Buddha the purest and most valuable of all
gifts: a small bowl of water.

—ANN JONES, "HIGH SOCIETY"

SHAPE OF THE PLACE

I THOUGHT FOR SOME REASON EVEN THEN OF AFRICA, not a particular place, but a shape, a strangeness, a wanting to know. The unconscious mind is often sentimental; I have written "a shape," and the shape, of course, is roughly that of a human heart.

—GRAHAM GREENE, *Journey without Maps*

VACATION IN MY OWN BACKYARD

W HEN I NEED A QUIET PLACE TO GO AND RELAX and be at peace with myself, it has to be to water. Water with sand. I lay back in the warm sand, nestling in, burying my body, my elbows, my heels. I lay back and listen to the lapping of waves against the shore, close my eyes and travel far away. I forget about the world, the heat seeping into every bone. My mind wanders and takes off onto journeys of its own.

I regret not being able to get away to a shore like this more often. I have entertained the thought of building a small pond in my back yard, surrounded by creamy white sand. That way, any time I need to escape, all I have to do is to step out my door.

—SUSAN BRADY, "GETAWAY"

A JOURNEY THROUGH HISTORY

*M*OST PEOPLE RETURN FROM EUROPE WITH A memory of the places they have visited that is very much like a salad after it has been put through a Cuisinart. They have been to so many countries and heard so many dates and names of kings that when they return, the trip is all a blur. When I see the typical American tourist, I feel like yelling out, "Don't do it that way, it's no fun. Do it my way."

If you do it my way, you will rent a time machine—available at any rent-a-car agency—and drive through history. Our time machine can't take us into the future any faster than a minute at a time, but we can, if we properly plan our route, actually simulate the sensation of traveling through several centuries of the past on a magical vacation in France.

—INA CARO, *The Road from the Past*

September 1

TARRAGONA, SPAIN

WE'VE TRAVELLED FAR, AND BEEF HAS BECOME mutton, chicken partridge—I should hardly know now if you gave me pork to eat. This is a sad state of things only balanced by the beauties of nature and the antiquities of man, upon which I would discourse if you would listen, but to tell the truth it is the food one thinks of more than anything abroad. When I tell you that the W.C. opposite our room has not been emptied for three days, and you can there distinguish the droppings of Christian, Jew, Latin, and Saxon—you can imagine the rest. This is Tarragona.

—VIRGINIA WOOLF, *Diary*

CROSS-COUNTRY REVELATIONS

*T*HERE IS SOMETHING ABOUT A JOURNEY THAT ONE takes with one's mother. It depends on the kind of relationship you have—it can either be a remarkable adventure or an extended period of displeasure. For me it was a gift.

After almost two years in Manhattan, I decided to move back to the Bay Area and I wanted to drive my car from Maryland to Oakland. My mother agreed to accompany me, either out of her own desire to see the country or because she didn't want to spend a week worrying about me on the road alone. I'd been living in a vertical cramped city and taking the time to drive across the States was to be a cleansing, transformative process for me. And it was. I felt myself stretch as we moved from Maryland to West Virginia and on to Ohio into Indiana and then Illinois. My soul lifted as the sunflowers turned and followed the sun and my car in Kansas. I wondered why so many people live in overpopulated cities when I saw all of the empty space in Colorado, Wyoming, Utah, and Nevada. And as we crossed the border into California, I realized that I was indeed home.

Not only was I transformed on this journey westward, but my relationship with my mom had also deepened and changed. We learned a lot about each other as the odometer rolled forward, and although she'd lost a daughter to the west coast, we both understood that we were now closer than ever.

—LISA BACH, "ROAD TRIP"

September 3

CONQUER YOUR DREAMS

EVERY SOVEREIGN PEAK OF THE WORLD, WHETHER Kilimanjaro in Africa, Mt. McKinley in North America, or Anconcagua in South America, Elbruz in Europe or Everest in Asia, is a challenge to the pioneering instincts of man. None quite so much so as the last, the Overlord of all mountains, which through our own generation and that of our fathers has been the symbol of remoteness and invulnerability. Perhaps it is this very fact which inspired the long series of brave struggles to attain it, struggles which became more determined and ever more gallant after man had reached both Poles and so left Everest as the last stronghold to be captured.

—COLONEL P. T. ETHERTON, ET AL,
First Over Everest! (1933)

September 4

TRAVEL TALES

*T*ONIGHT A SHEARED SLICE OF MOON HAS US MAD
to talk and watch as it makes its way over the great hill of
the sky…. Drinking kava makes us want to tell stories. I knew we
would tell stories eventually.

As we tell our stories, the beach fills with life, with passing
shapes lost in mist, and with color. The sand underneath us
becomes the vast and timeless desert of North Africa. The trees
above us creak and moan like the trees on the coast of India. A
wind blows up from New Zealand. Wind chimes in Burmese
villages whisper through the woods. Puffs of clouds off in the
distance and over the ocean become the Himalayas, the Andes,
the Urals, the Italian Alps. The people we describe in our stories come to life and sit here with us at the fire. Tales are spun
and woven deep into our souls. We listen spellbound, anticipating and dreaming of these places far away, these beautiful
mysterious places.

—LAURIE GOUGH, *Kite Strings of the Southern Cross*

September 5

WALKING INTO THE UNKNOWN

I ENTER A LAST STRETCH OF PITCH-BLACK ON THE dark north side of the hill. The slope steepens; I bend my knees and hips more, sinking down into my feet, relaxing the small of my back. Let go of the place that holds, let go of the place that flinches, let go of the place that controls, let go of the place that fears. Just let the ground support me. Listen, the wind is breathing in the trees. I hold my hand in front of me. It completely disappears. And yet I know it is there. The road bends to the right; I step off the solid, compacted dirt to the uncharted forest floor. My feet follow the edge of soft and hard, seeking out the trail through the dark tree tunnel.

Walking in the dark night is a way to practice faith, a way to build my confidence in the unknown. This faith is based both in what is known and what is unknown. I know how to walk forward; the motion is still the same in the dark. But by walking more slowly and carefully, my body makes room for what is not known. Each step is a small act of courage, a chance to practice with uncertainty. In walking into the blackness I learn the feeling of caution. I walk with the limits of what I can't see, guiding me, informing my steps.

—STEPHANIE KAZA, *The Attentive Heart*

AUSTRALIA'S NORTHERN TERRITORY

I DROVE TO MY CABIN AND ATTEMPTED TO open the door. It was locked. Assuming there must be someone in there I knocked and waited. Nothing happened. Assuming that whoever was in there could be sleeping off an NT stupor, I drove back to the bar and informed the young woman of my dilemma. "I'll send the manager," she said.

Once more I drove back to my room. A six-foot-something bloke wearing stubby shorts and sporting tree stumps for legs introduced himself as the manager. "She's locked, mate," he said after trying the door. "Yes, but I was told they only lock from the inside. There must be somebody in there," I replied. Without a word, the manager took a few paces back, paused for a second, and then ran furiously toward the door, raising his massive work boots to the handle.

The door flew open, the handle flew off and the window at the other end almost blew out. The room was empty. "She's open now," said the manager. That's what I call service.

PETER DAVIS, "ROOM CHECKING,"
Not So Funny When it Happened

September 7

CONTEXT OF THE WORLD

*T*O DREAM OF THE UNIVERSE IS TO KNOW THAT WE are small and brief as insects, born in a flash of rain and gone a moment later. We are delicate and our world is fragile. It was the transgression of Galileo to tell us that we were not the center of the universe, and now, even in our own time, the news of our small being here is treacherous enough that early in the space program, the photographs of Earth were classified as secret documents by the government. It was thought, and rightfully so, that the impact of our small blue Earth would forever change how we see ourselves in context with the world we inhabit.

—LINDA HOGAN, *Dwellings*

THE FACE OF FRANCE

*I*N THIS WHOLE KINGDOM THERE IS NO SUCH THING as seeing a tree that is not well behaved. They are first stripped up and then cut down; and you would as soon meet a man with his hair about his ears as an oak or ash. As the weather is very hot now, and the soil chalk, and the dust white, I assure you it is very difficult, powdered as both are all over, to distinguish a tree from a hairdresser. Lest this should sound like a traveling hyperbole, I must advertise your lordship, that there is little difference in their heights, for a tree of thirty years' growth being liable to be marked as royal timber the proprietors take care not to let their trees live to the age of being enlisted, but burn them, and plant others as often almost as they change their fashions. This gives an air of perpetual youth to the face of the country.

—HORACE WALPOLE,
LETTER TO THE EARL OF STRAFFORD (1769)

September 9

A Daring Adventure

$\mathcal{S}$ECURITY IS MOSTLY A SUPERSTITION. IT DOES NOT exist in nature, nor do the children of men as a whole experience it. Avoiding danger is no safer in the long run than outright exposure. Life is either a daring adventure or nothing.

—HELEN KELLER, *The Story of My Life*

A BALTIC MOTORCYCLE JOURNEY

*W*E FOLLOWED A SERPENTINE ROAD back toward the sea. It meandered like a sprung coil across ridges and valleys. Occasionally, the forest parted and revealed the blue vein of a stream, a meadow of bright summer grasses, the silver skin of a lake. A pure sapphire sky enveloped us. As we rode along I was grateful for the thousands of miles still to go.

Despite our weight and the bulk of our gear, the bike felt more like an appendage of our will to move than a distant machine. My hands knew just where to rest on the handlebars so I could coax the throttle with suggestions through my wrist. My feet were poised so the brake and gear levers were extensions of my toes. Each turn in the road was accomplished with an intuited shift of our torsos that sent us leaning toward the earth as we swept in precise arcs through them. The turning of the engine, the whirr of the tires on the road, the wind, were but the collective sound of our movement.

—ALLEN NOREN, *Storm*

September 11

DARJEELING, INDIA

*D*ARJEELING IS AN EXCEEDINGLY PRETTY PLACE, unlike anything I have seen before. It is laid in terraces on the side of the mountain. Looking down from the hotel, the streets form an interlaced and zigzag pattern. I should never know how to get to any given house in the place. It is like one of those labyrinth puzzles that you try to get to the center of without crossing a line. The safest way is to do as Alice did in the "Looking-Glass Hotel," turn your back to a place, and presently you find yourself walking in at the front door....

I like India better for having seen Darjeeling.

—LILIAN LELAND, *Travelling Alone* (1890)

UNDERSTANDING VIETNAM

SOMEWHERE BETWEEN THE PADDY FIELDS AND THE afternoons spent drinking tea with Tau, I found the Vietnam I had been looking for. In this tiny village not yet touched by the modern world, I discovered an ancient and universal celebration of community and family. I knew at last why I had come halfway around the world in search of this—because it had been lacking in me I would return with many memories—of an old man patiently shifting rocks to build a new field for corn; of the peace offering of a conductor for whom the past had become nothing more than a reason to share bread; of the women climbing hand over foot down a mountainside, balancing their loads with strong backs and serene courage; of a Zao patriarch who could look around and know that what he built would shelter his children and his children's children long after he had gone on to join the ancestors.

But most of all, I would take back a sense of place, an understanding of what I had left behind, and why it meant so much to me.

—KARIN MULLER, *Hitchhiking Vietnam*

September 13

SEA THE SOUTHWEST

*A*S I CRUISED AROUND NORTHEASTERN ARIZONA, I repeatedly had the sensation that I was traveling along an old sea floor. The landscape would seem to be thirsting for the water that had once been everywhere; the canyons would seem to plunge to murky depths; the mesas and monuments to be remnant shallows. Even the vegetation contributed to the illusion: sinuous wands of ocotillo wavered like seaweed, cacti bristled like sea urchins encrusted on the rock. Ship rocks—the ancient volcanic necks eroded in Gibraltar-like slants that crop up here and there on the Colorado Plateau—seemed to belong to a fleet sailing a ghost sea.

—ALEX SHOUMATOFF,
Legends of the American Desert

TAKING SIDES

*D*URING MY TWENTIES, WHEN I TRAVELED A GREAT deal, I became aware of a growing rift in myself. There was one side, and I identified it as male, that was eager to go into any kind of danger, and loved nothing more than to sit with a group of strangers, speaking a strange language, in the middle of nowhere. And there was another side, which I identified as female, that wanted only to stay home. I could hear their voices at different times, even at different times of day. The former I loved, for it longed for the rarest, most difficult stuff in life, the going beyond myself; but the latter, as the years went on, was becoming more emphatic, and more persuasive.

—SUSAN BRIND MORROW, *The Name of Things*

September 15

SAN FRANCISCO

*T*HERE IS A BLUFF IN THE PRESIDIO, TOWARDS the end of Washington Boulevard; some call it the Washington Bluffs, others Rob Hill, but it really has no name. There, at the sweeping curve of the road, you will find one of the finest views of the Golden Gate and the Pacific to be had anywhere. I always come back to this place, borne by the waves of sun and water that extend far beyond the boundaries of the eye, and reminisce about times long gone, dreams unfulfilled, and visions yet to be explored. An ancient Chinese couplet haunts me here:

> The moon in the water resembles
> the moon in the sky;
> The person in the heart is
> the person in front of you.

The sea- and pine-scented air fills me with hope and the belief that all men and women are made better by a visit to this place. The dream of San Francisco is that humanity might live in harmony with nature but at the same time enjoy the benefits of civilization.

Call to yourself down through the centuries and see if it is not here that you will return. San Francisco isn't just a city, it is a jumping-off point to eternity. In an ocean of light, this is the place.

—SEAN O'REILLY, "LADY OF THE AVENUES,"
Travelers' Tales San Francisco

ON THE TRAIL OF LOVE IN SPAIN

*H*E WAS BELGIAN AND HAD WALKED ALL THE WAY from his home. When Louella asked him why he was making the pilgrimage, he replied that he had worked as a schoolteacher for forty years and had been married for thirty-five of them. On retirement he found himself suddenly at home with a wife to whom he had nothing to say. Following the Way of St. James, he wrote to her each day and she to him at *postes restants*. It was, he said, like a honeymoon all over again and they were in love once more.

—ROBIN HANBURY-TENISON, *Spanish Pilgrimage*

September 17

A RIVER OF WORDS

 *T*HE FACE OF THE WATER, IN TIME, became a wonderful book—a book that was the dead language to the uneducated passenger, but which told its mind to me without reserve, delivering its most cherished secrets as clearly as if it uttered them with a voice. And it was not a book to be read once and thrown aside, for it had a new story to tell every day.

—MARK TWAIN, *Life on the Mississippi* (1883)

PARIS

I CANNOT TELL YOU WHAT AN IMMENSE IMPRESSION Paris made upon me. It is the most extraordinary place in the World. I was not prepared for, and really could not have believed in, its perfect direct and separate character. My eyes ached, and my head grew giddy, as novelty, novelty, novelty; nothing but strange and strik- ing things came swarming before me. I cannot conceive any place so perfectly and wonderfully expressive of its own character; its secret character no less than that which is on its surface, as Paris is. I walked about streets—in and  out, up and down, backwards and forwards—during the two days we were there; and almost every house, and every person I passed, seemed to be another leaf in the enormous book that stands wide open there. I was perpetually turning over, and never coming any nearer the end. There never was such a place for a description.

—CHARLES DICKENS, LETTER TO COUNT D'ORSAY (1844)

September 19

AFRICAN AWAKENINGS

*I*N THE MIND AND PERHAPS DREAMS OF EVERY PERSON
with black skin, the specter of Africa looms like the shadow
of a genie, dormant but not altogether harmless, always there,
heard about since childhood as some magnificent faraway
world, a place of magic and wonder. Africa as motherland.
Africa as a source of black pride, a place of black dignity. Africa
as explanation for the ways of black men and women, their way
of walking and their passion, their joys and their sorrows. Africa
as some germ in the genes that determines more than skin and
hair. Although I am not African, there is a line that connects that
place with this one, the place we come from and the place we
find ourselves, those lives and our lives.

—EDDY L. HARRIS, *Native Stranger*

RULES OF THE ROAD

*H*AD I TO GIVE A FEW UNIVERSAL RULES TO A young traveler, I should seriously counsel him thus: in Naples, treat the people brutally; in Rome, be natural; in Austria, don't talk politics; in France, give yourself no airs; in Germany, a great many; in England, don't spit.

—PRINCE HERMANN PUCKLER-MUSKAU (1785–1871)

September 21

TREKKING

ITHOUGHT UP THIS MOUNTAIN TRAVEL THING, which I called trekking. Trekking, of course, is a common word now, but then people didn't know. A Dutch word, really. Come from the Boers in South Africa. Just moving from one place to the other and stopping for the night. In those days trekking was the word commonly used for going to the base camp in an expedition. My feelings then were very different from adventure tourism, trekking tourism, nowadays. My idea was to attract the people who read all the books, you know, read Lord Hunt on Everest and what we did and things like that and thought, "Oh God, I wish I could go there myself and have this sort of adventure." And so I said, "Here we are, we'll lay it on for you." And of course I modeled the whole thing on what I knew first hand. I was on the British Everest expedition in 1953 as a sort of kitchen boy, and then was a full-fledged member of the American expedition in 1963. In 1950 I was the first Englishman in Pokhara and in 1956 made the first ascent by a foreigner of the Annapurna Sanctuary. Now you read about crowds of 200, 300 people going up. I suppose I was partly responsible for that.

—COLONEL JIMMY ROBERTS, *Travelers' Tales Nepal*

What's Wrong with Me?

I WAS SMITTEN WITH THE COUNTRY, ENCHANTED BY its sensuality. But this was no thanks to Italy's men. After two weeks in Italy, no men had pinched me. No men had harassed me. No men had spoken to me. Not a single one had even looked at me. I decided that I was the first and only young single American woman to travel in Italy who was not given the opportunity to endure or relish the advances of Italian men. I began to take it personally. At first I stopped trying to avoid eye contact with men. Then I began to seek it, to no avail. Soon I was wandering alongside Venice's canals, smiling at random men as I wondered what was wrong with me. Somebody bother me, please!

—Kristen Nesbitt, "Groping Italian Men"

September 23

SERENITY IN INDIA

"*I*'M LOSING MY SERENITY," I HISSED AT A BANK clerk after having spent all day trying to untangle currency problems which would have taken ten minutes to solve at home.

"Madam," he answered, "it takes many years to attain serenity. One does not lose it in a day."

—CHERYL BENTLEY, "ENCHANTED," *Travelers' Tales India*

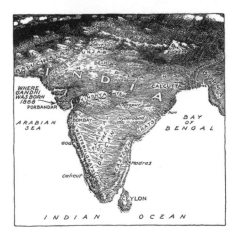

September 24

SHE'S ABROAD

OR MOST WOMEN, IMMOBILIZED AS THEY WERE by the iron hoops of convention, the term "abroad" had a dreamlike, talismanic quality. It conjured up a vision composed of a whole cluster of myths, half-myths, and truths—of sunlight, of liberty, of innocence, of sexual freedom, of the fantastic and the healing, of the unknown and the mysterious—all those concepts that stood in direct confrontation to domesticity. When women did buy tickets to sail on ships to India or to ride the Orient Express to Baghdad, their real destination, more often than not, was a restorative idea rather than a place on a map.

—LEO HAMALIAN, *Ladies on the Loose*

September 25

A ROYAL ABODE

*T*O THE TRAVELER IMBUED WITH A FEELING FOR THE historical and poetical, so inseparably intertwined in the annals of romantic Spain, the Alhambra is as much an object of devotion as is the Caaba to all true Moslems. How many legends and traditions, true and fabulous—how many songs and ballads, Arabian and Spanish, of love and war and chivalry, are associated with this Oriental pile! It was the royal abode of the Moorish kings, where, surrounded with the splendors and refinements of Asiatic luxury, they held dominion over what they vaunted as a terrestrial paradise, and made their last stand for empire in Spain. The royal palace forms but a part of a fortress, the walls of which, studded with towers, stretch irregularly round the whole crest of a hill, a spur of the Sierra Nevada or Snowy Mountains, and overlook the city; externally it is a rude congregation of towers and battlements, with no regularity of plan nor grace of architecture, and giving little promise of the grace and beauty which prevail within.

—WASHINGTON IRVING, *The Alhambra* (1832)

TRAVEL FOR ETERNITY

*S*O DO MEMORIES OF PLACES COME BACK, FOR IN spirit I shall ever revisit lands my eager, willing feet once trod. Surely it is worth something to have wandered in lands where the world's greatest have lived and left their traces. The sound, ripe fruit of contentment is mine—for traveling has ever been more than anything else—a passion so great it seems to me life beyond the grave will not be full or complete unless it be that Eternity means wandering from one fair world to another.

—MRS. WILLIAM BECKMAN, *Backsheesh* (1900)

September 27

TRAIN TRAVEL

*T*HE TRAIN DE GRANDE VITESSE BOUND FOR Marseille traveled so smoothly it was difficult to tell that we were moving at all. This smoothness did not diminish as the speed increased and I wondered why trains couldn't be like this back in Blighty. The difference between British and French tracks, I have since discovered, is that the French apparently have "superior technology." This baffles me somewhat. We are not talking about a closely guarded military secret or a tiny piece of micro circuitry in a laboratory, we're talking about lumps of steel nailed to bits of wood, and not only that but we're talking about something that is found in such abundance that I can't imagine anything easier than traveling to France, looking at the track, ascertaining what is different and copying it. However, this is apparently beyond the capabilities of those responsible for the British railway infrastructure, and that's just the way it is.

—STEWART FERRIS AND PAUL BASSETT,
Don't Mention the War!

AFRICA

AFRICA IS MYSTIC; IT IS WILD; IT IS A SWELTERING inferno; it is a photographer's paradise, a hunter's Valhalla, an escapist's Utopia. It is what you will, and it withstands all interpretations. It is the last vestige of a dead world or the cradle of a shiny new one. To a lot of people, as to myself, it is just "home." It is all these things but one thing—it is never dull.

—BERYL MARKHAM, *West with the Night*

DREAMING OF THE WORLD

*G*EOGRAPHY WAS ONE OF MY FAVORITE SUBJECTS IN school. From my earliest days, I have been mesmerized by maps, but I knew that no map—relief, topographic, or contour—could capture the richness, the sublime beauty, the smells, and variety of this earth. Even as a little girl, I was sure of that.

Books baited me even more. After reading about moors and mountaintop villages, igloos and trout-choked streams, I wanted to go out and see this world. Deciding to be a writer at ten cinched it; I believed it was my destiny to travel. A personal and professional imperative. Yet the more I learned about other countries and other peoples, the more overwhelming it felt. How can I understand it, if it is so big and mysterious? And so far away?

I wanted to travel to make the world more comprehensible, more familiar. I wanted to learn the dances the real Watusis did. I wanted to see if the Eiffel Tower was as tall as my father said. I wanted to go to sleep on a train and awake in another country.

I was a dreamer.

—DOROTHY LAZARD, "FINDING MYSELF IN THE WORLD"

INTO THE HEART OF CENTRAL AMERICA

I WANTED TO INFILTRATE, TO BE ABSORBED INTO, AND to absorb as much as possible the essence of that strange new place, however confusing and unwelcoming it might be. As I stood on the bridge, it seemed the most natural thing in the world to launch a boat and follow the rivers where they carried me, even necessary given their entry to the region's character— the quickest route to the heart of the country.

—CHRISTOPHER SHAW, *Sacred Monkey River*

October 1

BEHIND THE SHEET OF THE NIAGARA FALLS

*T*HE PATH WAS A NARROW, SLIPPERY LEDGE OF ROCK.
I am blinded with spray, the darkening sheet of water is
before me. Shall I go on? The spray beats against my face, driven
by the contending gusts of wind which rush into the eyes, nostrils, and mouth, and almost prevent my progress; the narrowing
ledge is not more than a foot wide, and the boiling gulf is seven-
ty feet below. Yet thousands have pursued this way before, so why
should not I? I grasp tighter hold of the guide's hand, and pro-
ceed step by step holding down my head. The water beats
against me, the path narrows, and will only hold my two feet
abreast. I ask the guide to stop, but my voice is drowned by the
"Thunder of Waters." He guesses what I would say, and shrieks
in my ear, "It's worse going back." I make a desperate attempt:
four steps more and I am at the end of the ledge; my breath is
taken away, and I can only just stand against the gusts of wind
which are driving the water against me. The gulf is but a few
inches from me, and, gasping for breath, and drenched to the
skin, I become conscious that I have reached Termination Rock.

—ISABELLA BIRD, *An English Woman in America* (1856)

THE VIEW FROM ABOVE

*D*AN AND I AGREED TO MAKE OUR ASCENT OF Mount Shasta slowly and not macho our way up and back in one day. After hiking two-thirds of the way up, we bivouacked for the night next to Lake Helen, a grimy puddle of icy water. We placed our tent in the middle of a ring of rocks others before us built for protection from the fierce winds. We cooked a light meal, chased tiny chipmunks away from our packs, then watched the sun set. Behind us the sun turned the cliffs blood red. The valley below grew dark, and we saw the lights of the town of Mount Shasta appear below. Campfires glowed in the dark canyons. Neither Dan nor I spoke, content simply to watch the dazzling show.

—MIKKEL AALAND, *The Sword of Heaven*

October 3

THE BLUE-GREEN SEAS OF FOREVER

*T*RAVEL IS METAPHOR, too, of the most idiotically simple kind. What are we doing when we travel? Crossing boundaries of reality, enlarging the spirit, exposing oneself to the unknown, discovering, being endangered, being infected, escaping, conquering, getting lost, forging a path, taking on the world, abandoning native origins, freeing oneself, asking questions, looking for something, finding oneself, going native, falling apart, experiencing the multiplicity of existence. Digging a tunnel to China. Sailing off on the blue-green seas of forever. Following a siren's call, following a drumbeat, getting away from it all.

—MICHELLE DOMINIQUE LEIGH, *The House on Via Gombito*

TIMELESS ADVICE

*N*OT THE LEAST IMPORTANT REQUISITE FOR A traveler is a ready stock of good temper and forbearance. Let your motto be, "Keep cool." Good humor will procure more comforts than gold. If you think you are imposed upon, be firm; custom has established certain charges; any deviation from them is soon detected, and, unless unnecessary trouble has been given, firmness and good temper will lower your bill more readily than violence.

Wherever you are, it is best to fall into the manners and customs of the place; it may be inconvenient, but it is less so than running counter to them.

—W. PEMBROKE FETRIDGE,
Harper's Handbook for Travelers (1862)

October 5

VILLAGE LIFE IN BALI

*W*E RENTED A MOTORBIKE AND TOURED THE back-country roads, driving along stunning beaches, through lush jungles, and up terraced hillsides with spectacular views of 10,000-foot Mount Gunung Agung and Penelokan Volcano. Everywhere we were unfailingly greeted with smiles. Early in the mornings, we laughed at the spectacle of peasants marching herds of waddling ducks in formation down to forage fields. There farmers impaled wooden poles, said to keep the fowl from wandering off. Outside the tourist areas, bronzed bare-breasted young women walked, balancing heavy baskets of vegetables on their heads. Of course, each village had its own stone temple, daily decorated with scarlet hibiscus tributes to the deities.

Approaching an isolated hamlet, we heard laughter and the echo of gongs. A cremation! How lucky we were, the only Westerners here. The dead man would progress to yet another life and the entire village was delighted for him. His body was carried atop a twenty-foot tower, spun round and round by the bearers to confuse any lurking evil spirit. In the process, a telegraph line was severed, shooting sparks into the air. I worried that the tower might catch fire, but the near calamity only accentuated everyone else's mirth. After all, the body was soon to be burned, and if the gods wanted to hurry the process, that was their will.

—DAN SPITZER, *Wanderlust*

OPEN SESAME

*M*OST OF US CAST LONGING EYES AT THE DOOR marked with the magical word "Europe," and it has opened freely enough when the husband said the "Open, sesame"; it is only of late years that women have made the amazing discovery that they can say it themselves with like success, but it is well to keep the hinges well oiled, and the rubbish cleared away from the threshold. When my turn came, I felt as if I had been taken into a high mountain and been promised all the kingdoms of the earth, and had at once accepted the offer.

—ELLA W. THOMPSON,
Beaten Paths, or a Woman's Vacation (1874)

October 7

BAKSHEESH

LOVE IT OR HATE IT, BAKSHEESH IS A WAY OF LIFE in Egypt. Almost everyone wants largesse in exchange for a service, even one as small as turning on a washroom tap. And, everyone has a favorite story.

My award for sheer gall goes to an old guy hanging around the Pyramids, who mooched a cigarette off me...then demanded baksheesh in return for lighting mine! But, as a practitioner of the art, he's left a country mile behind by the mounted policeman I met at the Citadel.

Sitting on a beautiful white horse, sternly mustached, dressed in immaculate whites, and caparisoned in *aiguillettes* and shining black leather, he was a picture waiting to be taken. "*Moomkin surah?*" (May I take a picture?) I asked. "*Inshallah!*" said the magnificent representative of Cairo's Finest, nodding in agreement.

God was indeed willing; I took my pictures and felt in my pocket for a small note for the customary "model fee." "No! No!" said the policeman, shaking his head. "Policemans must not take baksheesh!" Then he reached down, took the note and grinned. "Horse can take baksheesh!!"

—KEITH KELLETT, "BAKSHEESH,"
Not So Funny When it Happened

SIGHT AND SOUND ADVICE

*T*HE REAL FUN OF TRAVELING CAN ONLY BE GOT BY one who is content to go as a comparatively poor man. In fact, it is not money which travel demands so much as leisure, and anyone with a small, fixed income can travel all the time.

The beaten track is often the best track, but devote most of your time to the by-ways. In no other way can you so quickly reach the heart of a country. Yet, though I would have you do much of your journey by road, get a zest for traveling by railways. Just being in a train and rushing on to somewhere is extraordinarily nerve-soothing. Besides, a train goes through out-of-the-way places and enables you to surprise many intimate sights which you would miss from the highway. The track usually follows river valleys and a distraction can be found on a long journey in shooting the rapids in an imaginary canoe or in fishing likely pools. When there is no river, I take the hedges and ditches on a dream horse, or pretend that I am an airman and spot good landing places.

—FRANK TATCHELL, *The Happy Traveller* (1923)

October 9

GO VOYAGING

*I*T WAS EXHILARATING TO STAND ON THE BARRIER AND contemplate the sky and luxuriate in a beauty I did not aspire to possess. In the presence of such beauty we are lifted above natural crassness. And it was a fine thing, too, to surrender to the illusion of intellectual disembodiment, to feel the mind go voyaging through space... It could travel the universe with the audacious mobility of a Wellsian time-space machine.

—ADMIRAL RICHARD E. BYRD, *Alone* (1938)

THE CITY IS ALIVE

I AM ONE OF THOSE FOR WHOM THE VISIBLE WORLD exists, very actively; and, for me, cities are like people, with souls and temperaments of their own, and it has always been one of my chief pleasures to associate with the souls and temperaments congenial to me among cities.

—ARTHUR SYMONS, *Cities* (1903)

October 11

MELBOURNE, AUSTRALIA

 OMETIMES IN DREAMS THE FANCY CREATES A composite, colored photograph of a town, a place, or a house. The dreamer notices the difference of the component parts, but accepts the whole as correct... So it was to a certain degree with my impression of Melbourne. I saw it as a huge city in the Midlands of England, or the Five Towns, but the buildings were more perpendicular, the streets more rectangular, all was larger and more symmetrical, and there was a multitude of tramcars.

But these large, tall, black, square buildings were set in a soft, tepid, luminous air: pearly pink and gray...unlike anything in modern Europe—a dreamlike contrast.

When the fancy creates a place it forgets the necessary changes in background: air, sky, and light. This is true of dreams...

—MAURICE BARING, *Round the World in Any
Number of Days* (1913)

∽

Souls Touching

*A*T LUNCH ON MY FINAL DAY IN NAXOS, I ASK THE waiter where he is from. He replies shyly, "Lésvos." I ask about Sappho, which starts him talking, and I feel as if one of the Greek statues I've seen in the museum has come to life, a figure from an earlier time, eyes the color of the Aegean. And farseeing.

When he isn't serving others, he visits my tiny table, as grateful to talk about ideas and poetry as I am. When I get up to leave, he shakes my hand respectfully, saying, "My soul has been sore and empty for some time and needed filling." He speaks from the heart. Then he quotes Oscar Wilde, who spoke of "The quality of certain memorable moments." His big, rough farmer's hand shakes mine, and he says, "I get nostalgic for these talks I've had with people where for a few moments we've met, really touched."

The encounter was perhaps the greatest gift for me, the culmination of my stay in Greece.

—LILY IONA MacKENZIE, "THE ISLAND OF ARIADNE,"
Travelers' Tales Greece

October 13

INTO THE WOODS

IN NEW ENGLAND ONE WALKS QUITE GRADUALLY INTO a wood, but not so in the jungle. One steps through the wall of the tropic forest, as Alice stepped through the looking glass; a few steps, and the wall closes behind. The first impression of the dark, soft atmosphere, an atmosphere that might be described as "hanging," for in the great tangle of leaves and fronds and boles it is difficult to perceive any one plant as a unit; there are only these hanging shapes draped by lianas in the heavy air, as if they had lost contact with the earth. And this feeling is increased by the character of the earth itself, which is quite unlike the thrifty woodland floor at home; here the tree boles erupt out of heaped-up masses of decay, as if the ground might be almost any distance beneath. The trees themselves are so tumultuous and strange that one sees them as a totality, a cumulative effect, scarcely noticing details; there is a strange, evilly spined palm trunk, though, and a crouching plant with gigantic fronds, and a fantastic parasite, like a bundle of long red pipe cleaners studded with olive nuts, fastened here and there to the high branches, and the looming trunk of a silk-cotton, seen only when one is right on top of it; it soars off through the leathery green canopy overhead.

—PETER MATTHIESSEN, *The Cloud Forest*

WHAT IS REAL?

*W*E LOITERED ON THE CLIFFS FOR SOME TIME, leaning over them, and looking into the magic mirror that glittered there like a crystal, and with all the soft depth of a crystal in it, hesitating on the veiled threshold of visions. Since I have seen Aran and Sligo, I have never wondered that the Irish peasant still sees fairies about his path, and that the boundaries of what we call the real, and of what is for us the unseen, are vague to him. The sea on those coasts is not like the sea as I know it on any other coast; it has in it more of the twilight. And the sky seems to come down more softly, with more stealthy step, more illusive wings, and the land to come forward with a more hesitating and gradual approach; and land and sea and sky to mingle more absolutely than on any other coast. I have never realised less the slipping of sand through the hour glass; I have never seemed to see with so remote an impartiality, as in the presence of brief and yet eternal things, the troubling and insignificant accidents of life. I have never believed less in the reality of the visible world, in the importance of all we are most serious about. One seems to wash off the dust of cities, the dust of believes, the dust of incredulities.

—ARTHUR SYMONS, *The Aran Islands* (1896)

TRIUMPH ON MOUNT EVEREST

*T*O MY RIGHT A SLENDER SNOW RIDGE CLIMBED UP to a snowy dome about forty feet above our heads. But all the way along the ridge the thought had haunted me that the summit might be the crest of a cornice. It was too late to take risks now. I asked Tenzing to belay me strongly and I started cutting a cautious line of steps up the ridge. I wave Tenzing up to me. A few more whacks of the ice axe, a few very weary steps and we were on the summit of Everest.

My first sensation was one of relief—relief that the long grind was over; that the summit had been reached, that in the end the mountain had been kind to us. But mixed with relief was a vague sense of astonishment that I should have been the lucky one to attain the ambition of so many brave and determined climbers. It seemed difficult at first to grasp that we'd got there. I was too tired and too conscious of the long way down to safety really to feel any great elation. But as the fact of our success thrust itself more clearly into my mind I felt a quiet glow of satisfaction spread through my body—a satisfaction less vociferous but more powerful than I had ever felt on a mountaintop before.

—Sɪʀ Edmund Hillary, *High Adventure*

October 16

ATHENS, GREECE

"**P**EOPLE RUSH THROUGH ATHENS ON THEIR way to the islands," he said, "and take in nothing but the Acropolis." Antonis recited the words of a shepherd he'd encountered while lost in the mountains: "A foreigner and a blind man are the same. They don't see what's in front of them." And it's true—Athens has gotten a bad rap among travelers, for its traffic jams, overcrowded tourist sites, and seasonal air pollution. But there is another side to Athens, and those who focus only on the city's glorious past, Antonis says, are missing its seductive present: its sensual dry heat and sea light; its blue sky and bright flowers; the icy drinks, garlicky dips, and tangy cheeses served in cafes; the splashes of green and, everywhere, a citrusy smell; the startling hills that jut up heroically in the center of town.

—ALAN BROWN, "ATHENS, LOOK CLOSER"

October 17

FERNANDO PO, EQUATORIAL GUINEA

SEEN FROM THE SEA, OR FROM THE CONTINENT, IT looks like an immense single mountain that has floated out to sea…and anything more perfect than Fernando Po when you sight it, as you occasionally do from faraway Bonny Bar, in the sunset, floating like a fairy island made of gold or of amethyst, I cannot conceive. Its moods of beauty are infinite; for the most part gentle and gorgeous, but I have seen it silhouetted hard against tornado clouds and grandly grim. And as for Fernando Po in full moonlight—well there! You had better go and see it yourself.

—MARY KINGSLEY, *Travels in West Africa* (1897)

A PELICAN FRENZY

*W*E HAD DRIVEN A VOLKSWAGEN OVER THE high mountains from Oaxaca to the coast. It took us six long hours and we were hot and out of steam when we arrived at the lazy Mexican beach resort of Puerto Escondido. I jumped into my swimsuit the minute we got into our room and headed for the beach. The cool water was gloriously refreshing.

Suddenly, I felt my foot hit a fish and then the ocean began to explode around me. I froze with fear.

I looked up and saw a hundred pelicans swarming down on me. Some were landing as close as two feet away. Splashes were erupting everywhere, and in the center of this hysteria I realized that they were swooping in on a school of fish and I was in the middle of a feeding frenzy.

Then understanding replaced panic and I watched in awe as pelicans scooped up fish with what appeared to be gallons of water.

I dove down to see what this chaos looked like from beneath the surface and the exploding noise was muffled immediately. The water erupted with turbulence as a pelican dove down next to me, snatched up one of many silver flashes and then propelled himself upwards with strong webbed feet. I have no idea how long this frenzy lasted, but when it finally ended it stopped as suddenly as it had begun. I yelled and waved my arms in excitement. I felt alive and vital, but mostly I felt privileged to have shared such a moment with these magnificent birds.

—PAMELA CONLEY, "A PELICAN FRENZY," *The Gift of Birds*

IN THE VALLEY OF NAPA

*W*INE IN CALIFORNIA IS STILL IN THE EXPERIMENTAL stage; and when you taste a vintage, grave economical questions are involved. The beginning of vine-planting is like the beginning of mining for the precious metals: the wine-grower also "prospects." One corner of land after another is tried with one kind of grape after another. This is a failure; that is better; a third best. So, bit by bit, they grope about for their Clos Vougeot and Lafite. Those lodes and pockets of earth, more precious than the precious ores, that yield inimitable fragrance and soft fire; those virtuous Bonanzas, where the soil has sublimated under sun and stars to some thing finer, and the wine is bottled poetry: these still lie undiscovered; chaparral conceals, thicket embowers them; the miner chips the rock and wanders further, and the grizzly muses undisturbed. But there they bid their hour, awaiting their Columbus; and nature nurses and prepares them. The smack of Californian earth shall linger on the palate of your grandson.

—ROBERT LOUIS STEVENSON,
The Silverado Squatters (1883)

TRAVEL CHANGES YOU

*H*ERE'S WHAT I LOVE ABOUT TRAVEL: STRANGERS get a chance to amaze you. Sometimes a single day can bring a blooming surprise, a simple kindness that opens a chink in the brittle shell of your heart and makes you a different person when you go to sleep—more tender, less jaded—than you were when you woke up.

—TANYA SHAFFER, "LOOKING FOR ABDELATI,"
A Woman's Passion for Travel

October 21

TWO KINDS OF SILENCE

*T*HERE ARE TIMES WHEN I LOVE JAPAN'S SILENCES. Away from the din of urban Japan, deep in a bamboo grove, the ground thick with leaves, I swear you can *hear* the stillness. Then a breeze stirs, and it's like the whole world breathing, the swaying of the bamboo, synchronized, inhaling and exhaling, like a sigh.

I've had moments exactly like that with some of my Japanese friends. *Ishin denshin*, wordless heart-to-heart communication: there's nothing like it.

At other times Japanese silence is a prison. You know there's something inside, desperate to break out, but language, culture, and tradition are powerful jailers. The most you will see is a scrawny arm waving desperately from between the bars.

—CATHY N. DAVIDSON, *36 Views of Mount Fuji*

A JOURNEY INTO BHUTAN

*T*HE SCENERY CHANGES ALMOST EVERY TIME WE turn a corner. Shadowy pin, sunlit oak and beech, dry, hot groves of subtropical pine, called "chir pine" accord to Rita, dense, moist jungly forests. Sometimes the mountains roar up, steep and black and haughty. Other times they are more gentle, sprawling, spreading, dissolving into haze. In these I can trace profiles, a smooth forehead, an aquiline nose, a stubborn chin. Whenever we stop and climb out of the vehicle, I am struck by the silence. It is particularly deep and strong higher up. At the passes, when the wind drops suddenly, the silence almost hums, and I can feel the weight of the earth beneath me, intensified by the emptiness between this solid piece of ground and the nearest ridge, a short flight away. It becomes a strange mental gravity. If I stand too long, I begin to feel rooted.

JAMIE ZEPPA, *Beyond the Sky and the Earth*

October 23

LET YOURSELF GET STRANDED

A COUNTRY LOOKED AT FROM THE SEA IS LIKE the sleeping Princess, the unknown. From the land it is no longer enchanted, but varied and human, a foundation for friendship and living. And perhaps it is a good way to come to know it when machinery breaks down and one is left marooned in a quiet place, one's own life suspended in a vacant interval that human variety can wander through at will.

—FREYA STARK, *Alexander's Path*

THE CHANGING FACE OF TRAVEL

*W*E WERE MEANT TO MOVE. OUR ANCESTORS WERE wanderers, hunters, and gatherers. They followed herds and water. They relocated themselves continuously, depending on the weather and seasons. Our very survival once depended on our mobility. On every continent, tribal communities traveled to where the best opportunities lay—they moved or they died. To this day, we carry this legacy within our genes, programmed over millennia.

Travel has certainly changed over the years, from walking and riding horseback to sitting in bullet trains and supersonic jets. The reasons people travel have evolved considerably as well. Conquest, nomadic wandering, and religious pilgrimage are no longer prime motives for most of us. Still, whether in ancient Babylon or the Australian Outback, people used to travel for many of the same purposes we do today: to explore the world, to find better opportunities for work and trade, or to seek romance and adventure.

—JEFFREY A. KOTTLER, *Travel That Can Change Your Life*

October 25

ALLURING NEPAL

I AM OFTEN ASKED, "DID YOU LIKE NEPAL?"—TO which I usually reply, "Yes" and leave it at that. But no one merely "likes" Nepal; Nepal weaves a net out of splendor and pettiness, squalor and color, wisdom and innocence, tranquillity and gaiety, complacence and discontent, indolence and energy, generosity and cunning, freedom and bondage—and in this bewildering mesh foreign hearts are trapped, often to their own dismay.

—DERVLA MURPHY, *The Waiting Land*

A GIFT TO A STRANGER

"JEANS. HAVE YOU ANY JEANS?"

In the fascination of young Russians for Western things, jeans are the *ne plus ultra* of the modish, cult, and modern. They can be sold for eight times their London price. Yes, I had a pair of new British jeans.

"New?" His face fell. He had hoped I owned an old pair. He was too poor to buy new jeans at black market prices. He was married with one daughter, he said, and couldn't even afford a second child. He opened the door and prepared to plunge back into the rain.

"Take the jeans for their English price," I said.

As he stared at me, his eyes grew watery with gratitude. Only later did I reflect that I was offering him the equivalent of a month's salary. "Oh please, yes," he said weakly, "yes, yes…." His fingers laced and unlaced under his neck like the forelegs of a mantis.

—COLIN THUBRON, *Where the Nights are Longest*

October 27

ALASKA

NYONE WHO HAS EVER BEEN TO ALASKA remembers the light. There is sometimes too much of it, and sometimes not enough. The land seems to be in a perpetual state of sunrise or sunset. There is always a pink-blue glow in the sky. Trees are silhouetted. Clouds and mountaintops are often rimmed with golden sunbeams. Even after dark, there is magic in the sky.

—ANN MARIAH COOK, *Running North*

THE HARMONY OF THE WILD

*N*IGHTS IN AFRICA ARE NEVER SILENT. IF YOU LISTEN carefully an entire orchestra of diverse sounds and secret voices reaches you from the grass and the hills, the dunes, the ponds, and the trees. And if you look for the unseen creatures which animate the night you can often, for a moment, glimpse their eyes, piercing the blackness.

—KUKI GALLMANN, *African Nights*

October 29

STEP FORTH AND BEYOND

*T*O THOSE BRED UNDER AN ELABORATE SOCIAL order, few such moments of exhilaration can come as that which stands at the threshold of wild travel. The gates of the enclosed garden are thrown open, the chain at the entrance of the sanctuary is lowered, with a wary glance to right and left you step forth, and, behold! the immeasurable world. The world of adventure and of enterprise, dark with hurrying storms, glittering in raw sunlight, an unanswered question of an unanswerable doubt hidden in the fold of every hill. Into it you must go alone, separated from the troops of friends that walk the rose alleys, stripped of the purple and fine linen that impede the fighting arm, roofless, defenseless, without possessions.... So you leave the sheltered close, and, like the man in the fairy story, you feel the bands break that were riveted about your heart as you enter the path that stretches across the rounded shoulder of the earth.

—GERTRUDE BELL, *The Desert and the Sown* (1907)

MEMORIES OF SAN SEBASTIAN

*T*HE STONEWORK STREETS IN THE OLD SECTION OF town were wet, the cold accentuated by the dense shadows cast by ancient tall buildings. We wandered through these narrow antique corridors, amazed by the architecture, the strangeness of the Basque language on the signs, looking for warmth. All of a sudden we turned a corner and the iconic architecture of a cathedral completely filled the narrow frame at the end of the  street. It was like coming out of a dark tunnel into the expansive light of day. We forgot the cold. Suddenly we could understand the implicit importance of the church to the Basque people. We looked up and there it was. It was as if we were lost, and seeing it were found.

—JUDY ROSE, "SAN SEBASTIAN,"
Love & Romance

October 31

GIBRALTAR

*A*ND OH, WHAT A GLORIOUS UNIVERSE—AFRICA and Europe and the Atlantic and the Mediterranean, flooded in starlight at my feet—the tiny blazing ships far below creeping east to Suez—the sleeping sloping city on one side; on the other a sheer precipice from the top of which I could drop a stone into the phosphorescent breakers nearly one thousand four hundred feet below—northward was Spain and the Sierras; southward the jagged crest of this wonderful Rock as it sagged and rose once more to a point even higher than my own. The Straits of Gibraltar were turned to silver by the moon. The African Pillar of Hercules, so clear and so close, rose yet another one thousand feet above me. The stars in the heavens met the stars in the harbor. It was Paradise even without the jug of wine.

—RICHARD HALLIBURTON,
The Royal Road to Romance (1925)

November 1

MISADVENTURE

I HAD A FRIGHTFUL MISADVENTURE THIS MORNING. Last night, on going to the English mission for an injection, I was thankful to accept their kind suggestion that, since the doctor was away, I should sleep in his bedroom. In the middle of the night the poor man came back unexpectedly, and seeing a strange head on his pillow, was obliged to sleep on a sofa. But worse followed. When at last he did venture into his own room to fetch some clean clothes, he caught me in an orgy, sitting on his bed over a bottle of wine and a cigar. Knowing I should be out all day, I was lunching early. I tried to put a bold face on it by offering him some wine, but he formed an unfavorable impression.

—ROBERT BYRON, *The Road to Oxiana*

November 2

KATHMANDU

*T*HE ENERGY OF THE PLACE SLAMS LIKE A SHOCK wave... Kathmandu is so overwhelming, so packed with images, that succinct summaries seem almost impossible—certainly inadequate. I'm tempted to say "You'll understand when you get there...." It's a dream. I've never seen anything like it.

—DAVID YEADON, *The Back of Beyond*

TOTAL SOLAR ECLIPSE, CHILE

I'M HIDING OUT AT A BEND IN THE ROAD HIGH IN THE Chilean altiplano, waiting for a total solar eclipse. My boyfriend and I have been here for three days. "Don't move, someone's coming," we periodically whisper, crouching lower behind the sheltering boulders. Only no one ever comes this far. We're too high up, the air is too thin. Walking, even just one curve of the road, exhausts. We understand; we don't want to move either.

"*Adios*," we called to the manager of the *refugio* three days ago, slinging on our packs. In an effort to protect Parque Nacional Lauca from the thousands of eclipse-chasers recently descended upon northern Chile, the park has been reserved for select tour groups only—not us. But after months of eclipse planning and dreaming—from Venezuela through Colombia, Ecuador, Peru, and Chile, bus ride after bus ride—we couldn't bear to go. Not only had we reached the ideal longitude and latitude for this event, this spot, along the shores of Lago Chungara, at the foot of a dormant volcano, had taken hold of us.

So, here we are. Distanced from the *refugio* by one bend in the road, seeing but unseen, eating what food remains, witnessing the most spectacular sunsets of our lives, we wait. It won't be long now. In just an hour, sun, moon, and earth will face one another, fire to rock to sea, and for one brief, exquisite moment morning will turn to night. And we will stop hiding.

—NATANYA PEARLMAN, "WAITING FOR THE ECLIPSE"

November 4

VIETNAM

*B*USING IN VIETNAM IS A FREEWHEELING ENTERPRISE, somewhat akin to the stagecoaches of the old American West. Privately owned buses, driven by the owners and their relatives, go bumping from town to town hailing freight, livestock,

and produce and picking up riders standing on the side of the road like hitchhikers. A stripped-down traveling show, they roar along, working every minute, shooting from village to village, laughing and cajoling a livelihood from the highway boredom. They haul on a skeleton crew of four—any more and there are too many mouths to feed, any less and they're liable to be cheated by their customers. The driver is always and only the driver, keeping his eyes on the road and muttering prayers to the Buddha mounted on the dashboard. There couldn't be a more serious lot of drivers in the world. These guys deal in life and death daily, their whole family riding on their performance, the bus their vehicle, the whole family's savings and possibly their coffin on wheels. In my brief travels here, I've seen several dead buses, smashed, rolled belly-up, and disemboweled by salvagers.

—ANDREW X. PHAM, *Catfish and Mandala*

A KILLARNEY STORM

*T*HE WEATHER IN THE EARLY HOURS OF THE following morning was unusually fine. The blue of the sky was perfectly clear and placid, and yesterday's storm was only a reminiscence. It had swept over Killarney town with great severity, and hailstones had fallen which the natives said were "as big as small p'taties." But it was the thunder rather than the hailstones that had  especially aroused the anxiety of the townfolk, and their alarm was of much the same type as that I had witnessed in the hut on the mountain. They did more praying in the short duration of this one storm than they would have done in six months of fair weather, and with every crash from the heavens the sins of the whole community were repented of afresh.

When the storm passed the praying ceased, and I suppose no more wholesale repenting was done until there was another thunderstorm.

—CLIFTON JOHNSON, *The Isle of the Shamrock* (1901)

November 6

TOLEDO, SPAIN

*W*E HAVE BEEN TRAVELING FOR HOURS THROUGH a country filled with an immense energy—with the energy of silence. The enormous plain stretches out to the blue horizon's hound; it is brown as dust, it is grey and ashen, but with the changing hours the colors change. It is mauve and it is *réséda*, it is sage green and periwinkle blue; and set in the midst thereof, and fair as a star sapphire, and so old that age is nonexistent, is the city. Time has no power upon her beauty, which was ordained before time was. The twilight of the ages is luminous upon her; she broods, aloof and fair, a place of enchantments. As Spain has no dew, so Spain has no dreams, but she has magic, and some of it is black magic; as Siena is a city of dreams, so Toledo is a city of enchantments, legendary and magical.

—GEORGIANA GODDARD KING, *Heart of Spain*

A DREAM FULFILLED

*W*ITH THE WIND IN MY HAIR AND WATER FROM the Pacific splashing up on the sides of our boat, I smiled with the realization that my first travel dream was coming true.

Australia had always been a distant dream, one planted in me by my grandfather. His stories of diving had inspired me and, although he'd never been to the Great Barrier Reef, he believed it was the best. I always dreamed of one day going.

We were in the middle of the ocean, with no landmarks in sight. The captain anchored, and I was the first one in the water. What looked like just another dark blue ocean surface revealed a different world below. A school of silver and black striped fish encircled me and when they cleared, I saw a seven-foot shark swimming ten feet beneath me. He was considered a baby, and although our guide had assured me that the sharks were harmless, I stayed close to the boat until he glided out of view.

The uneasiness passed fairly quickly as I watched fish swim in and out of the coral caves. I dove down to get a closer view of rainbow colored parrotfish nibbling on the arms of golden coral. The coral was like none I'd ever seen before—circular orange tables and lavender flower blossoms. The loud steadiness of my breath in the snorkel was the bass rhythm to the fish performing their choreographed dance in the reef. I wanted my grandfather to be there with me, with the reef below us, our dreams coming true together.

—JENNIFER LEO, "A WORLD BELOW"

A JOURNEY

*D*OES THE ROAD WIND UPHILL ALL THE WAY?
Yes, to the very end.
Will the journey take the whole long day?
From morn to night, my friend.

—CHRISTINA ROSSETTI (1830–1894)

PALERMO, ITALY

I SUPPOSE PALERMO, THE GREAT BAY OF PALERMO
with its lofty promontories thrust out into the sea, so noble
in outline and in mass, Monte Pellegrino on
the west, and Monte Alfano on the east, the
city set as it were in a natural amphitheatre
between them on the shore of the blue
jewel-like sea, its palaces and turrets and
minarets seen against the dark background
of far flung mountains, and surrounded by
the riches of all vales, the Conca d'Oro,
running up in an ever narrowing valley into
the great bare hills, with its olive gardens,
its orange and lemon groves, its fig trees
and almonds, its palms and agaves and its infinite flowers: I
suppose Palermo is one of the loveliest places in the world.

—EDWARD HUTTON, *Cities of Sicily* (1926)

November 10

THE DEAD SEA

*T*HE SEA WAS SPREAD OUT BEFORE ME, MOTIONLESS
as a lake of molten lead. The sand is not bright like that of
an Atlantic or Mediterranean beach, but of a dirty, dark brown.
The water is exceedingly clear and transparent, but its taste and
smell are a compound of all that is bad....

Before I left Jerusalem I had resolved not to bathe in it, on
account of my health;... but, on the point of turning up among
the mountains, I could resist no longer. My clothes seemed to
come off of their own accord, and before Paul had time to ask me
what I was going to do, I was floating on its waters. Paul and the
Arabs followed, and, after splashing about for a while, we lay like
a parcel of corks upon its surface.

—JOHN LLOYD STEPHENS,
Incidents of Travel in Egypt (1837)

HIGH ABOVE THE RAGING MALANA RIVER

*O*UR HEAVY BACKPACKS UPSET OUR BALANCE, BUT WE made it to the middle of the cliff, both of us hanging just above the torrent.

Then I moved too soon. For one long minute, with my foot on top of Michael's, neither of us able to move, I thought I'd fall and drown. I started to panic. I tried not to look down, but I was morbidly fascinated. Would the current bash me against the rocks, or could I paddle to shore? Could I even paddle wearing a backpack? It must have been about this place that Dervla Murphy wrote: "I wondered whether my imminent death would come from a broken neck on the rocks or through drowning…" Tears of fear and self-pity smarted my eyes. Then I remembered to breathe slowly and I imagined I was on solid ground. I lifted my boot, freeing Michael's trapped foot. As I hung over the seething river by just one foot and three fingers, I experienced the greatest concentration of sheer terror I've ever felt.

On the other side of the rock the path started up nonchalantly, almost innocently. We didn't know whether to congratulate ourselves for our daring or to chastise ourselves for our poor judgment, but there was time for neither. For a moment we stared at the river thundering hungrily down its bed of boulders and felt strangely part of it.

—MARY ORR, "THE VALLEY OF REFUGE,"
Travelers' Tales India

INTO THE DEEP WILDERNESS

WE GO INTO THE WILDERNESS WITH OUR WHOLE selves. It asks no less of us. It asks the utmost of our bodies. It asks that we perceive it with accuracy. The price can be high if we do not.

If we look intently we find a great deal more than we knew we would find. Scientists have accumulated a vast hoard of facts and know that they still may not have more than pricked the mother lode of knowledge. But if facts are all they perceive, they have not yet learned wisdom.

In the wilderness wisdom comes on the wind and in the stillness; it shows us ourselves, our deepest, archaic, forgotten, and truest selves. We recognize that we are of the Earth and of the Universe—a part of the structure, and it is within us and of us—inseparable.

—MARGARET P. STARK, *How Deep the High Journey*

HAUNTED CANYON

*S*OARING 1,700 FEET FROM THE GROUND, Shiprock, New Mexico, can easily be seen as the mythical "rock with wings" that its Navajo name, *Tse'Bit'Ai* implies. Legend has it that the rock was once a bird that had carried the Navajo to northwestern New Mexico. Settling to the ground at the death of the day, sundown, it took on the guise of a rock. Geologists will counter that story with a clinically factual account that it was a volcanic plume that was part of a much higher plateau, at the same level as nearby Mesa Verde. As the soft earth eroded, the plume became the monument that it now is.

Whichever version of its origin you prefer, Shiprock is an impressive natural feature and, when viewed at the close of the day, takes on the guise of the *Tse'Bit'Ai*. It is understandable why it has such a place of reverence in Navajo lore and why it is spiritually uplifting. Viewing Shiprock from any angle, distant or near, it rises from the earth with a majesty that only Nature can endow on a feature.

—DAVID ROBERTS, "BIRD OF THE DESERT"

November 14

RAIN DANCE

*W*E'RE IN THE PICOS DE EUROPA, NORTHERN, huddled inside a tiny cider house. From out of the rain, four small women in blue rain ponchos burst into the room. Their hoods come down, and they shake out tousled graying hair—laughing, talking rapid Spanish, making friends with everyone. Andalusian women, of course. Open from the sunshine that they enjoy in the south nearly year-round, unlike the mountain people here in the north, who are closed like the half-shut crocuses that grow here.

Later, when we're all in the parking lot boarding our tour buses, the rain halts. In an instant, the four Andalusians begin to clap their hands rhythmically, and then to sing. Their arms fly into the air and their hands swirl like little birds, and suddenly those women who are well into their sixties are transformed into sensual creatures, dancing the *sevillana* in the middle of a parking lot. It is only a brief moment; then the rain begins again and the blue hoods go up, and the women scurry to their bus, their laughter reaching back to us through the rain.

—LUCY MCCAULEY, "TOURING SPAIN"

A SENSE OF ITALY

*T*O THE AMERICAN, ESPECIALLY IF he be of an imaginative temper, Italy has a deeper charm. She gives him cheaply what gold cannot buy for him at home, a Past at once legendary and authentic, and in which he has an equal claim with every other foreigner. In England he is a poor relation, whose right in the entail of home traditions has been docked by revolution. But Rome is the mother country of every boy who has devoured Plutarch or taken his daily doses of Florus. Italy gives us antiquity with good roads, cheap living, and above all, a sense of freedom from responsibility.

—JAMES RUSSELL LOWELL,
Leaves from My Journal in Italy and Elsewhere (1854)

November 16

ENCOUNTERING A *NACANACA*

"WHAT IS IT?" SHE REPEATED. I COULD NOT answer. I knew my life lay in her hands, and whatever she did to save me she must do alone, and without the slightest mistake. She did not have a flashlight, for it had been lost overboard one night, and she was unarmed. Besides that, she was a rotten shot. I will not deny that I was thinking intently and I am not ashamed to say that I was thinking of God, in a completely detached way, and I was wondering if on death you saw Him, or if it was a light you saw—or if death was like dreaming in sleep, or utter unconsciousness, or absolute blackness. I felt with certainty that this was the end of the individual ego of one Leonard Clark, that he was nothing but a mass of chemicals to be used over and over again, and that from that moment on, he was in the hands of whatever force was moving the atoms and the worlds.

With the other half of my brain I heard Inez move. Any moment she would see the snake through my netting in the beam of my flashlight—would she scream....

The sweat was trickling down my face, and I was holding my eyes as still as I could, staring into the black eyes only a few inches away. Next I felt something move under my head and knew it was her hand, feeling for my gun. The hand slowly withdrew. At least a full minute must have passed—the big automatic roared alongside my head, and the snake struck.

—LEONARD CLARK, *The Rivers Ran East*

THE NILE

*T*O THOSE WHO WISH TO BE WISE, TO BE HEALTHFUL, to borrow one month of real pleasure from a serious life, I would say, come and see the Nile.

—H. M. STANLEY,
My Early Travels and Adventures (1869)

THE WEIGHT OF FREEDOM

"*W*ELCOME TO MIAMI, FLORIDA," THE PILOT said, "*Free* Territory of the Americas." They cheered again, even louder than before.

To my surprise, I felt like cheering, too. I had been in Cuba only twenty-three days and unaware of any great pressure, but what lifted from my shoulders in that moment was a very heavy weight. The busybody comrades of the Defense Committees, the dresser drawer-rifling secret police, the marches blaring from loudspeakers, the Big Brother slogans, the sense of menace were all behind me, and America was just ahead.

I was to have the same feeling again in years to come—on taking off from Saigon and escaping the war in Vietnam, and on getting out of pre-glasnost Russia, and on leaving brutal China behind me in the midst of the Tiananmen Square uprising. The peace of the twenty-third Psalm settled upon me, the part about still waters and green pastures and the soul restored.

I felt released. I felt light as air.

—CHARLES KURALT, *A Life on the Road*

ICELAND

*T*HERE IS SOMETHING ALLEGORICAL ABOUT THE very fact of Iceland, something that puts most visitors in mind of still remoter grandeurs —Dantean visions of heaven or hell, or classical conceptions of Elysium, improbably transplanted to these icy realms with asphodels among the glaciers. This is an island of absolutes, where nothing is blurred, and sometimes it feels less like a country than a prophecy, a mystery play, or a topsy-turvy sort of Utopia.

—JAMES MORRIS, *Places*

November 20

BEING PRESENT

*M*Y PASSION FOR TRAVEL STARTED AS A YOUNG girl. I read. I disappeared into words and images and places that introduced love and pain and possibility. I traveled to places in my head with the longing of one who's lost a lover, yet I'd never known one. I chose the college I went to based on their study abroad program. But even as I studied in England and traveled to Paris and Moscow and loved it all, I felt as if I was missing something. Something was unsettled, like a poem I had yet to understand.

After college I moved to San Francisco and a year later I headed east, on bicycle, toward Yosemite. There is a stretch of road that winds back and forth, gradually making its way up the steep incline of the Sierra range. I shifted gears and pedaled slowly along the white line that marks pavement's edge, unsure of my strength after a few long days of hauling a loaded bike. Gradually, granite and shrubs became pine. I lifted my head at that moment and saw the land and the sky and the friend riding in front of me; I felt the world around me in a way I'd never experienced before. A moment of inclusion and elation, of belonging in the world and feeling my small place in it. Recognizing that it's not about escaping or leaving but about being present, here. There were no drums or shouts to announce this moment, instead there was silence, just me and the road and the sun and the air. I felt more alive than I had ever felt.

—MICHELLE HAMILTON, "THE GIFT OF TRAVEL"

AMAZON TRADING

I BOARDED OUR BOAT TAKING US UP THE AMAZON River to the Amazon Lodge. The next morning we were led on a narrow trail through the jungle by our guide to visit a village of Yagua Indians. Just twenty years earlier, they had been dangerous head-hunters, and I remember being appalled at seeing small, black shrunken heads hanging from their windows. We watched Yagua men

demonstrate blowing poison darts through long blow guns. I was unprepared to trade with the Indians, and rummaged through my purse to find something to trade. I found an old mirror and held it up to bargain. Immediately, a small brown woman with a wrinkled face came towards me, pushing her husband forward to do the negotiating. As she peered into the mirror, her dry cracked face broke into a wide smile with few teeth, instantly transforming her into a young shy girl. She said something to her husband unintelligible to me, and he presented me with a necklace made of seed pods. I took the necklace and placed it around my neck. We both nodded heads and they stepped away. The bargain was sealed and completed.

—PAMELA CONLEY, "IN THE AMAZON"

THE YANGTZE RIVER

*A*LL CHINESE KNOW THEY ARE FED BY THE YANGTZE and flooded by the Yangtze; they know the river is their country's gateway and its major highway; they write poems about it and sing songs to it, they fight battles on its banks, they sign treaties on its shores, they draw water for fishing and washing and making power, they dump rubbish in it, they drown babies in it, they scatter ashes in it and pollute it with coal and sulphur and naphtha and the excretion and decay of every animal known, and of humans too. They respect it, fear it, welcome it, run from it, hate it and love it. More than any other river in the world—more than even the Nile, which also cradles an entire country and nurtures a civilization—the Yangtze is a mother-river. It is the symbolic heart of the country, and at the very center, both literally and figuratively and spiritually, of the country through which it so ponderously and so hugely flows.

—SIMON WINCHESTER,
The River at the Center of the World

A LOST CHANCE ON LOVE

I WONDERED WHETHER MY LIFE WOULD EVER BE THE same after this day. I felt as if I'd known Pilar all of my life, but had no idea if I would ever see her again. I wanted to believe that her life, too, would be irrevocably altered by our meeting

We made our way up Madrid's Paseo del Prado to the Puerto del Sol. We elbowed our way through the crowd of shoppers who filled the square. We wandered up Calle de Preciados and enjoyed playing the parts of young lovers. We even went into one shop and tried on engagement rings.

At the train station, when it was time for me to return to London, Pilar walked with me onto the platform. As she stood there, her smile fading for the first time since I had known her, she reached into her handbag and pulled out a book of poems by Pablo Neruda and recited—all I can remember of it is this line, in her voice:

Look for me for here I will return, without saying a thing, without voice, pure, here I will return to be the churning of the water, of its unbroken heart....

That was many years ago now. But hardly a day goes by that I don't think about Pilar. I wonder why I didn't stay with her and live out the romance. I wonder if she is sitting in a café in Madrid, looking across the square for me.

—GLENN A. LEICHMAN, "LOOKING FOR PILAR,"
Travelers' Tales Spain

November 24

BELOW THE SURFACE IN THAILAND

I CLIMBED TO THE SUN DECK TO WATCH BANGKOK from the river as I had so often watched the river from Bangkok. The life of Bangkok is on its waters and it was on the

river that I had always sensed the real heart of the country. The bulk of the people in Thailand were like the ones who clustered on the banks of the river or who paddled on it in their teak craft and these were the people with whom no *farang* ever talked beyond, perhaps, a few words of bargaining. When any Westerner tells you that he knows the East like a book and pretends to be an authority, beware, for he is lying. Even the Westerners who stay for years rarely penetrate below a certain class in the East. They meet the Westernized, the cultured, and the rich and always behind this shallow façade are the numberless Siamese they cannot begin to comprehend and who are Thailand.

—CAROL HOLLINGER, *Mai Pen Rai Means Never Mind*

FROM PLACE TO PLACE

*A*LL OF US WANDERERS ARE MADE LIKE THIS. A good part of our wandering and homelessness is love, eroticism. The romanticism of wandering, at least half of it, is nothing else but a kind of eagerness for adventure. But the other half is another eagerness—an unconscious drive to transfigure and dissolve the erotic.

We wanderers are very cunning —we develop those feelings which are impossible to fulfill; and the love which actually should belong to a woman, we lightly scatter among small towns and mountains, lakes and valleys, children by the side of the road, beggars on the bridge, cows in the pasture, birds and butterflies. We separate love from its object, love alone is enough for us, in the same way that, in wandering, we don't look for a goal, we only look for the happiness of wandering, only the wandering.

—HERMANN HESSE, *Wandering*

CONSUMING ITALY

*T*HERE IS NOTHING LIKE THE SMELL OF A *TRATTORIA* in Rome. Italian restaurants elsewhere have as much relation to a Roman *trattoria* as pornography has to great sex.

In Rome when the doors to a *trattoria* are opened, in one grand sniff the meal is revealed in the small mosaics of its parts, similar to the way an overture gives you a musical sample of what is to come. Prosciutto, salami, garlic, onions, oregano, wine, coffee, bread, olive oil, fresh white linen, vinegar, vigorous noise and convivial clatter, stone, dampness, marble, and almonds chorale into libidinousness which is stopped, (but no one realizes it) by the formality of the place and the starch and snap of the waiters.

—GEORGE VINCENT WRIGHT, "CUISINE SAUVAGE,"
Travelers' Tales Italy

A FINE DAY AT THE AUSSIE BEACH

*T*HE BEST THING ABOUT CAPE TRIBULATION IS THE sand on the beach. It's very, very fine. The finest. It gets all over you: in your hair, on your skin—practically inside your pores. But the thing is you don't mind. You actually kind of like the rough-smooth feeling of countless tiny, clean grains scraping lightly across the back of your hands, your fingertips tickling almost electrically.

And that fine, fine sand never really leaves you. Maybe in a few months or years, when you've forgotten all about it, you'll absently rub the back of your neck and you'll feel a gentle rustle. You'll take your hand from your neck and see, caught in the whorls of your fingertips, tiny pieces of beach sand. You'll remember being on the beach at Cape Tribulation and you will remember being happy.

—SEAN CONDON, *Sean & David's Long Drive*

November 28

Thanksgiving in Nepal

OUR CAMPSITE WAS AT 16,000 FEET, AT A PLACE called Lobuje, two days' trek below Everest Base Camp. By then we had been walking for three weeks, up from the sunny green rice terraces of the Hindu lowlands, up past the Buddhist monasteries with their prayer wheels turning, to this place of ice and rock and a few yaks groaning in frozen pastures.

We knew that at home, it was Thanksgiving, and home was very far away. Dinner that night was the usual salt-dried shrimp and noodles. The cook, hearing that it was a special holiday for us, came up with a special dessert: canned mangoes, shortcake, and rum sauce—which quickly inebriated us all in the thin air. Squatting in the mess tent, I longed to dine at a real table, for warmth, for level ground, for my mother's face.

Later, I lay shivering in my sleeping bag. Somewhere off in the night our Sherpa porters were chanting, dancing their strange stomp-shuffle dance. I thought about how it was on the other side of the world. Millions were gathering around tables for a uniquely American feast. The roasted brown bird, the cornbread dressing, fresh tart cranberry sauce, pumpkin pie—oh, Lord, I could smell it, taste it, roll the red wine on my tongue, hear the jovial talk.

Now, all these years later, those days on the trail to Everest are clearer to me than yesterday. And I believe that was the most delicious Thanksgiving dinner of my life—the one in my dreams of home.

—Lynn Ferrin, "Nepali Dreams"

Don't Touch

I AM VERY AWARE OF HANDS IN THIS COUNTRY. IN Vietnam it is impolite and unseemly to touch strangers. Most people don't even observe the Western custom of shaking hands. Children will sometimes touch you as you walk by, out of childish curiosity at some one who looks nothing like them or theirs. Or they will run up from behind, touch you and flee. But they're just playing a game of "counting coup." They know it's naughty, but the fascination of foreigners overcomes their good manners. Or they might be pickpockets in training. But certainly an adult who touches you on the street is at least being disrespectful, and could be trying to get your goods.

—Richard Sterling, "Turning the Tables,"
Testosterone Planet

November 30

MOSCOW, RUSSIA

"*T*HE HISTORY OF THE KREMLIN IS THE HISTORY OF Moscow and Russia itself," Natasha said as we walked through the Kremlin's Trinity Tower, past the fifteenth century walls of the medieval fortress and into Russia's very heart…. "Outside the Kremlin's fortifications, scores of wooden houses, churches, and shops sprouted in rings around the citadel. Inside the Kremlin, the city within a city, each successive ruler left his or her mark, until the Kremlin's sixty-six enclosed acres contained a half-dozen of the country's most sacred cathedrals, numerous palaces, nineteen towers, dungeons, secret passageways, and the Terem, or woman's quarters, a medieval palace of parapets, stained-glass windows, gilt ornamentation, and intricately painted interiors straight out of *One Thousand and One Nights*."

We strolled through Alexandrovsky Garden and into Red Square. Here was the Moscow I'd known of, instantly familiar from photographs: GUM, the nineteenth century shopping arcade; the Kremlin Wall and Spassky Clock Tower; Lenin's Tomb and the Lenin Historical Museum. St. Basil's Cathedral appeared at the far end as a shimmering chimera, its twisted towers and painted domes undulating in the heat waves that rose from Red Square's ancient cobblestones.

"So," Natasha turned to me, "what do you think?"

"Walt Disney on acid," I said.

—CHRISTI PHILLIPS, "WORKING FOR RUBLES"

COLORS OF AMERICA

*O*NLY THE OTHER DAY, TAKING THE NIGHT TRAIN from Chicago to New York, I felt myself all but overcome by the sheer human grandeur of the United States. After dinner in the restaurant car I walked back through the darkened coaches to my sleeper, as the great train labored across the continent toward Cleveland, Toledo, Buffalo, and Albany, over many a gleaming river and through many a slumbering hamlet. Lurching and swaying I made my way back, coach after coach, and as I went I saw to the right and left of me, exposed in the innocence of sleep, the faces of young America. They were black, and brown, and white, and yellow, some more handsome than others, some scrunched up against seat backs, some thrown back with open mouths; but seen as a whole that night, as we plodded on across the continent, they moved me with a most poignant sense of beauty—the beauty of the American idea, really. Few of those travelers were old, none of them were rich, or they would not be traveling coach class on Amtrak; some lay in each others' arms and one had a pet turtle—sleeping, too—upon his chest; sentimentalist that I am, it brought the tears to my eyes to see them.

—JAN MORRIS, *Pleasures of a Tangled Life*

≈

December 2

AMBOISE, FRANCE

A LITTLE WHITE-FACED TOWN, STARING ACROSS AN admirable bridge, and leaning, behind, as it were, against the pedestal of rock on which the dark castle masses itself. The town is so small, the pedestal so big, and the castle so high and striking, that the clustered houses at the base of the rock are like the crumbs that have fallen from a well-laden table.

—HENRY JAMES, *A Little Tour in France* (1882)

FOR THE LOVE OF TRAVEL

*W*E TRAVEL, INITIALLY, TO LOSE OURSELVES; AND WE travel, next, to find ourselves. We travel to open our hearts and eyes and learn more about the world than our newspapers will accommodate. We travel to bring what little we can, in our ignorance and knowledge, to those parts of the globe whose riches are differently dispersed. And we travel, in essence, to become young fools again—to slow time down and get taken in, and fall in love once more.

—PICO IYER, "WHY WE TRAVEL"

December 4

MONKEYING AROUND

*A*T UYENO PARK...I SAW A MOST AMUSING MONKEY. It was chained to the fence. In the little crowd that gathered around, quite out of the monkey's reach, was a young Japanese boy, who, in a spirit of mischief, tossed a pebble at the red-faced mystery, who turned with a grieved and inquiring air to my friend.

"Go for him," my friend responded. The monkey turned and with its utmost strength endeavored to free itself so it could obey the bidding. The [child] made his escape and the monkey quieted down, looking expressively at the place where the [boy] had stood. The keeper gave the monkey its dinner, which consisted of two large boiled sweet potatoes. The monkey greedily ate the inside, placing the remainder with the other potato on the fence between his feet. Suddenly he looked up, and as quick as a flash he flung, with his entire force, which was something terrific, the remaining potato at the head of someone in the crowd. There was some loud screaming and a scattering, but the potato missing all heads, went crashing with such force against a board fence that every particle of it remained sticking there in one shapeless splotch. The [child], who had tossed the pebble at the monkey, and so earned his enmity, quietly shrunk away with a whitened face. He had returned unnoticed by all except the monkey, who tried to revenge himself with the potato. I admired the monkey's cleverness so much that I would have tried to buy him if I had not already owned one.

—ELIZABETH COCHRANE SEAMAN, *Nellie Bly's Book* (1890)

THE MAGIC STONES OF ANGKOR

*J*UNGLE, JUNGLE, FOR MILE AFTER MILE ON EVERY SIDE it smothered the earth, dense, black, consuming—and from out of it, unheralded and unbelievable, rose the gigantic, the magical temple with its tier on tier of gray tapestried stone, acres of carving, hundreds of delicately-wrought windows, miles of galleries, great lace towers—all powerful and beautiful and desolate beyond imagination.

The spectacle was so amazing, stumbled on here in the forest, I would have scarcely credited my eyesight had I not been prepared by the fleeting distant glimpse of it snatched over the tree-tops early that morning. To have blundered upon the Pyramids or St. Peter's, suffocating in the jungle depths of this wild corner of Asia and utterly deserted but for bats and lizards, would not have astonished me more—indeed not nearly so much, for Angkor, built by gods for a fabulous vanished empire, in the might of its dimensions, in artistry, in purity, in magnificence, and above all in preservation, Angkor surpasses anything Greece or Rome or Egypt has ever seen.

—RICHARD HALLIBURTON,
The Royal Road to Romance (1925)

December 6

THE NIGHT SKY

*T*HE CARLSBAD CAVERNS ARE A PART OF THE mountain ranges in the Chihuahuan Desert. It is the summer home of millions of Mexican free-tails bats. Man reached here, in the 1800s, led by the bats. Settlers were drawn into the caverns by the phenomenon of millions of bats, issuing from the caves and surging in the sky.

After I spent the whole day in the Pecos River, my eyes ached for soothing darkness and nocturnal life. Dusk settled. A small group of people waited in gathering darkness. We sat in utter silence, as if anticipating a miracle. Beyond the familiar surroundings of rugged mountains, of uneven plains, away from sunlight and birds, away from men and machines, yawned the cave in a weird land.

Then, from the silence of subterranean chambers rises a tumultuous sound, like a wind rumbling, roaring through a rain-drenched forest, like ancestral voices from the land of the dead. Like stones hurled from an underground fountain, come dark beings from the mouth of the cavern. The fountain rises higher and higher, a dark moving mass of flapping wings and squeaking creatures. A sunken river of black pours into the sky, like a tide leaping upward. Time stands still. The gigantic swarm hangs silhouetted against the night sky—a dramatic display not meant for man. In less than two hours, the black tornado winds its way across the sky like a huge serpent. And there, it disappears in the southeast, into the night.

—PADMA JAYARAJ, "THE CARLSBAD CAVERNS"

MEETING THE LOCALS

"*I* HAVE ALWAYS RELIED ON THE KINDNESS OF strangers" may be a traveler's mantra, but it's the hitch-hiker's maxim.

The following vehicles stopped to pick up this lonely traveler in Iceland: a cement truck, a white Renault, a blue Opal, a black Fiat Uno, a battered white Lada (driven by a Brooklyn-raised mathematics professor), a NATO school bus (I refused), and an oversize delivery truck, twice.

The delivery truck first picked me up at the T-junction between Keflavík, Reykjavík, and Grindavík. Two days later, in an extraordinary occurrence of kismet, it stopped for me again along the Vesturlandsvegur highway, 75km to the east. Sævar, the truck's owner, suffered from the very unIcelandic condition of ebullience. He offered me air-cured herring and onions, and a warm can of Coca-Cola to wash it down. "It's gooood," he thundered, and thumped his chest. Because of Sævar I have had the grand tour of Kópavogur suburb ("where the rich people live!"), where I saw the national library, the president's house, the hospital where he was born, and the Viking restaurant where they serve decomposed shark meat and roasted sheep's head.

In Iceland, where bus service is haphazard, distances vast and weather mercurial and mostly cold, the kindness of strangers is warming indeed.

—Q WILLIAMS, "HITCHHIKING ICELAND"

December 8

SAGE ADVICE

*F*INALLY, A WORD OF WARNING. THOUGH THE MAP might show a good short cut from here to there, follow principal, well-marked roads. It may be an adventure but rarely fun for long to find yourself faced by several forks of country road in a sea of olive trees; no signs, no one to ask, and daylight fading.

—KATE SIMON, *Italy*

MAP JOURNEYS

*O*N EVERY MAP THERE ARE CERTAIN NAMES THAT possess deep mystery. Some names are as beautiful as elegant women: Iferouâne, a desert oasis in the Sahara; Januária, a city on the São Francisco in eastern Brazil; Ivalo, in Finnish Lapland on the south shore of Lake Inari. Some names tell you of the tragedy and dashed hopes of settlers: Badwater, Destruction Bay, Deadhorse, Bete Grise; some tell you of the hilarity and cockeyed optimism of those very same settlers: Chicken Rock, What Cheer, the Pourquoi Pas glacier. The names on maps are pictographs, compact narratives composed of only one or two words, and through them we travel without leaving our own doors: they tell us the stories of those who wandered and those who claimed; those whose thirst was slaked by a provident spring and those whose children died along the road; and those who with great joy first saw a new land, its green fields, its deep forests, its birds like airborne prisms, its hills a territory of endless wonder.

—LAURA HARGER, "INSIDE THE MAP"

December 10

RUSSIA

THE FIRST QUESTION EVERYONE ASKS YOU ON YOUR return from the Soviet Union is: "Were you followed?" Every Western tourist likes to think he was. There is really no fun going to a police state if you're not followed by someone. In the Hotel Metropole in Moscow I had the feeling I was always being watched, but it was always by other tourists who thought *I was watching them.*

—ART BUCHWALD, *More Caviar*

LOCH KATRINE, SCOTLAND

*T*HE SUN HAD BEEN SET FOR SOME TIME, WHEN, being within a quarter of a mile of the ferryman's hut, our path having led us close to the shore of the calm lake, we met two neatly dressed women, without hats, who had probably been taking their Sunday evenings' walk. One of them said to us, in a friendly and soft tone of voice, "What! You are stepping westward?" I cannot describe how affecting this simple expression was in that remote place, with the western sky in front, yet glowing with the departed sun.

—DOROTHY WORDSWORTH, *Journal* (1803)

December 12

KANCHEJUNGA

I ARRIVED IN DARJEELING IN A DENSE FOG. ABOVE THE window in the living room of the teahouse was a panoramic photograph of the most magnificent mountains I had ever seen. I asked where the scene was. The proprietor tilted her head as if I were nuts and pointed out the window. "There," she said.

I looked out at the solid bank of clouds and vowed to stay as long as necessary to see that sight. Each morning I'd wake up and eagerly look out my window but it was always the same gray mist, until one morning I awoke at dawn and sensed something different in the texture of the sky visible from my bed. My heart started to race. I sat up and there, filling the window and most of the sky was the glimmering massif of Kanchejunga, dusted a brilliant red by the rising sun and sprawling across the horizon as if embracing the whole world. For many moments I disappeared into it, overcome by the sheer gravity of the mountain. It was the most powerful vision I'd ever seen.

—LARRY HABEGGER, "STROLLING TO SIKKIM,"
Travelers' Tales India

THE LOVE OF PLACE

*A*ND I LOOKED UP AND SAW THE MOUNTAINS across the bay, knife shaped, coloured, & the sea, brimming, smooth, & felt as if a knife had scraped some incrusted organ in me, for I could not find anything lacking that agile, athletic beauty, steeped in colour, so that it was not cold, perfectly free from vulgarity, yet old in human life, so that every inch has its wild flower that might grow in an English garden, & the peasants are gentle people; & their clothes, worn & burnt, are subtly coloured, though coarse. Now there are sympathies between people & places, as between human beings. And I could love Greece, as an old woman, so I think, as I once loved Cornwall, as a child.

—VIRGINIA WOOLF, *Diary*

SAVIORS IN HIGH PLACES

*T*RIPS OVERSEAS USUALLY INVOLVE INTERMINABLE air travel, with bad food, talkative seatmates, and never enough room to stretch your legs. Feeling grubby and exhausted from my red-eye international flight, I boarded my six A.M. connection from Amsterdam to Milan. I left behind my American airline and was now seated in a European carrier. Suddenly, my impression of flying had completely changed.

Smiling flight attendants greeted me and, as soon as we were airborne, delivered steaming hand towels, followed by orange juice and fresh baskets of warm muffins. It was an ethereal, hallucinatory experience after the previous twelve hours. The sun was now bright outside my window, I was wide awake, and in a short time I would be wandering the streets of Milan. Thanks to the angels in the air, I was again a believer.

—ERICA SMITH, "ITALIAN AWAKENINGS"

OF MULES AND JAMAICA

*I*F YOU GO TO JAMAICA YOU ARE GOING TO WANT TO visit the Maroons at Accompong. They are under the present rule of Colonel Rowe, who is an intelligent, cheerful man. But I warn you in advance not to ride his wall-eyed, potbellied mule. He sent her to meet me at the end of the railroad line so that I would not have to climb that last high peak on foot. That was very kind of Colonel Rowe, and I appreciate his hospitality, but that mule of his just did not fall in with the scheme somehow. The only thing that kept her from throwing me was the fact that I fell off first. And the only thing that kept her from kicking me, biting me and trampling me under foot after I fell off was the speed with which I got out of the way after the fall. I think she meant to chase me straight up that mountain afterwards.

—ZORA NEALE HURSTON, *Tell My Horse*

THE SOUTH SEA ISLANDS

*T*HE SOUTH SEA ISLANDS HAVE AN INVINCIBLE
glamour. Any bar in 'Frisco or Sydney will give you tales
of seamen who slipped ashore in Samoa or Tahiti or the
Marquesas for a month's holiday, five, ten, or twenty years ago.

Their wives and families await
them yet. They are compound,
these islands, of all legendary
heavens. They are Calypso's
and Prospero's isle, and the
Hesperides, and Paradise, and
every timeless and untroubled
spot. Such tales have been made
of them by men who have been
there, and gone away, and have been haunted by the smell of the
bush and the lagoons, and faint thunder on the distant reef, and
the colours of sky and sea and coral, and the beauty and grace of
the islanders. And the queer thing is that it's all, almost tire-
somely, true. In the South Seas the Creator seems to have laid
Himself out to show what He can do. Imagine an island with the
most perfect climate in the world, tropical, yet almost always
cooled by a breeze from the sea.

—RUPERT BROOKE, *Letters from America* (1916)

BORDER CROSSINGS

*S*OMEHOW I MANAGED TO MAKE IT BACK THROUGH the cordon between Guatemala and Costa Rica unscathed. Eventually it all blurs into one seemingly endless border crossing, punctuated by occasional bouts of movement. At each one a flurry of Important Papers are distributed, then traded for cash or the currency of the hour—or, more often, a stack of U.S. one dollar bills. At each we are confronted by a noisy gaggle of moneychangers pressed tight against the bus door, each one brandishing fistfuls of multicolored bills. At each one sits the same gang of bored officials, the same vendors hawking the same gristly grilled chicken, the same skinny dogs darting about nervously, all seemingly transported from one border to the next. Guatemala. El Salvador. Honduras. Nicaragua.

—BRENDAN POWELL,
"TRAVELS THROUGH CENTRAL AMERICA"

December 18

A SECRET MAP

*I*N THE RECESSES OF HIS IMAGINATION EVERYONE, I believe, must carry a secret map given him in childhood with the sites of treasure troves marked upon it where the rest of the world sees only a town's name; and to travel is to try and reach these sites, pickaxe in hand, hoping against hope for the ring of its blade on the buried casket. So, wakening early to the feelings of a boy on his birthday, I pulled open the curtains and saw, beyond the roofs of the town, the shining waters of the Euxine. Trebizond! The pick stuck gold.

—PHILIP GLAZEBROOK, *Journey to Kars*

ON THE ROAD

*Y*OUR ROAD IS EVERYTHING THAT A ROAD OUGHT TO be…and yet you will not stay in it half a mile, for the reason that little, seductive, mysterious roads are always branching out from it on either hand, and as these curve sharply also and hide what is beyond, you cannot resist the temptation to desert your own chosen road and explore them.

—MARK TWAIN (1835–1910)

December 20

LEAVING PARIS

I FOUND PARIS ESPECIALLY DIFFICULT TO LEAVE THAT morning. Familiar buildings and monuments glistened with fresh snow that had fallen during the night. Teary eyed, I almost fell as I skidded over the medieval cobblestones of my Marais apartment courtyard. The taxi driver studied me disapprovingly in his rear view mirror.

"Why are you leaving Paris?"

"Because I must return to my job and home in San Francisco."

"Tsk. Tsk," the ultimate French negation, and a slow-motion head shake registered his displeasure.

"What matters most in life is that you make love with someone you care about on Sunday morning and walk out with them on Sunday afternoon. It's not good to live your life alone."

—DIANE LEBOW, "THE TROUT BARON"

TRAVEL WITHIN

$\mathcal{M}$ ANY PEOPLE THINK WE TRAVEL TO RUSH OUT into crowds of people, but most of us travel to travel within. There is no more quiet and central space than the anonymity of being in a foreign place without ties or obligations.

In quiet moments sitting alone at a café, looking down on a village from the edge of a cliff, or in the suspended peace of a soaring cathedral, we can pause to look back with objectivity and forward with intelligence and hope. Travel can be a series of these small epiphanies. With distance we can see patterns, themes, and questions our life has posed to us, and sometimes, in a faraway place, the answers come.

—JUDITH BABCOCK WYLIE, *Love & Romance*

December 22

A Man's Best Friend in the Arctic

*A*FTER A DAY OF HIGH LIVING ON THE ONE CARIBOU ham, eight bear-paws, and five Canada jays, we were down to a diet of skins and oil again. We also ate our snow-shoe lashings and several fathoms of other raw-hide tongs—fresh rawhide is good eating; it reminds one of pig's feet, if well boiled. It occurs to one in this connection (seriously speaking) that one of the material advantages of skin clothing over woolens in Arctic exploration is that one can eat them in an emergency, or feed them to one's dogs if the need is not quite so pressing. This puts actual starvation off by a week or so. As for eating one's dogs, the very thought is an abomination. Not that I have any prejudice against dog-meat, as such; it is probably very much life wolf, and wolf I know to be excellent. But on a long, hard sled trip the dogs become your friends; they work for you single-mindedly and uncomplainingly; they revel with you in prosperity and good fortune; they take starvation and hard knocks with an equanimity that says to you: "We have seen hard times together before, we shall see good times again; but if this be the last, you can count on us to the end." To me the death of a dog that has stood by me in failure and helped me to success is the death of a comrade in arms; to eat him would be but a step removed from cannibalism.

—VILHJAMUR STEFANNSSON, *My Life with the Eskimo* (1913)

LAOS

*L*AST YEAR AT THIS TIME I was traveling in Laos. I spent my birthday and Christmas in the small riverside village of Nong Khiaw. Food was scarce and I was lucky to be able to find a bowl of noodles. I was feeling one of those lonely pangs of homesickness one sometimes gets on the road, often during holidays, wondering what my friends and family were doing.

Just at that moment this small girl ran up to give me a beautiful pink flower, a gift from the universe. She didn't want anything in return, just handed it to me with a grin, and ran away. It's the most wonderful birthday gift I've ever received, and I still look at it taped in my journal, a reminder, that sometimes the simplest gifts are the most precious.

—ALISON WRIGHT, "A SIMPLE GIFT"

December 24

BAJA

O NE OF MY PASSIONS IS THIS MAGNIFICENT peninsula that we often call "The Baja." Its deserts are beautiful and dangerous and full of mysteries and stories. Its seas are abundant. Over 500 species of plants and animals are unique to it. Its history is tortured and full of brave hearts and big dreams and mighty failures. Its tiny little town of Mulege is the only recurring mark on my calendar. The week from Christmas to New Year usually finds me here, though I come here whenever else I can as well. Its transpeninsular highway, twisting for a thousand miles, is the symbol of my other great passion: the road. The great, long road to all the world. It is where I live, in the fuller sense of the word. It is where stories are most alive. It has lead me around the planet several times. I've followed it down dank alleyways and up grand boulevards; into mansions and into humble huts; into the company of the sacred and the profane, and into the innumerable stories that make up my life. Stories of Baja, and stories of far away. For these things my passion never cools; and for this I am always alive. The fire never dies. I always feed it anew.

—RICHARD STERLING, *The Fire Never Dies*

December 25

HOLIDAY ABROAD

CHRISTMAS IN NORTHERN THAILAND, FRESH OFF A trek and a million miles from home. Our guesthouse is planning a Christmas party to take place in the flower-filled courtyard where we gather for meals. When we return from a trip to the night market the place is transformed with colorful streamers and candles. Presents are hidden in the vines and creeper and we pick numbered chits and rush off to find our gifts. Ripping them open we discover handmade bags in jewel-toned Thai silk, small baskets, and other local novelties. A feast is laid and we savor the exquisite flavors of the Thai soups, curries, and vegetables. We discover mangosteen, creamy, sweet segments nestled in a dark purple skin, and gorge ourselves on papaya, pineapple, watermelon, and jackfruit. We talk and laugh and eventually sing, dredging up carols from Christmases past, and the courtyard resounds with a mixture of accents from around the world. Our Thai guides, now friends, reciprocate with haunting tunes of their own as the candles burn low. Finally, the *piece de resistance*, a Christmas cake, a *real* Christmas fruitcake is brought out. Ordered from Dublin by the Irish woman who, with her Thai husband, co-owns the guesthouse, it is delicious. Filled with dried fruit and covered with marzipan frosting we sink our teeth into this amazing confection. It is the best Christmas cake we have ever tasted. Here, far from those we love, we feel surrounded by friendship and joy. It is an unexpected gift, long treasured.

—TARA AUSTEN WEAVER, "CHRISTMAS IN CHIANG MAI"

December 26

THE LONG ACRE

*O*NCE IN A WHILE THE FEELING COMES BACK, THE craving for the air of Connemara and the walks at dusk down the long acre, the stonewall-lined roads along the seaside.

Winter, years ago. Vagrant memories of living on Irish fry breakfasts, potatoes and beer, the melancholic sweetness of rosewood fiddles and bodhran drums, and lusty nights along the twilight edges of the Celtic world. Hitchhiking under slate-gray skies, trying to read the poetry of sullen megalithic stones and fathom the fabled melancholy of the ancient land of my ancestors.

On I traveled through Ireland's "soft days" of gentle rain, with *soul clapping*, as Yeats wrote from his stone tower; rambled on under *the heaventree hung with nightblue fruit*, as Joyce rhapsodized in cunning exile; ventured on *into the slipstream*, as Van Morrison sung from Hynford Street. Each night, in a different inn along the road, I wrote to faraway friends and distant family to convey my astonishment that I had escaped the hellhounds of the hometown factories and been blessed with the chance to live as if I were truly *alive*.

Those cards and letters, dropped into magic lantern mailboxes, and franked with brilliantly colored stamps, revealed a heart bursting with happiness. Across the sea my words flew, shaped like seagulls riding the thermal winds over the Cliffs of Moher, words sailing on winds of sheer joy, flying as far as they could.

—PHIL COUSINEAU, "IRELAND"

KENYA, AFRICA

*L*IFE IN KENYA, WITH ITS EXTRAORDINARY BEAUTY and variety of opportunities, its unbounded space and spectacular landscapes teeming with wild animals, its lakes and deserts, mountain ranges and countless beaches, its savannah, forests and windswept Highlands, attracts people of an unusual quality, who regard risk and challenge as an intrinsic part of the safari of existence. They fly with the moonlight and land in the dark; they hunt alone for lion and buffalo in thick bush, or for crocodile, wading waist-deep into rivers and lakes; alone they climb deceiving mountains; they explore on foot waterless deserts and forbidding country where bandits are known to attack travelers; they dive in shark-infested waters, or sail with light craft in turbulent seas; they defy malaria, yellow fever, and tropical disease; they approach dangerous animals to study or film them. They gaily court danger, and, although a number of them perish, quite a few manage to survive.

—KUKI GALLMANN, *African Nights*

December 28

RISK AND REWARD

*S*LIPPING, FALTERING, GASPING FROM THE EXHAUSTING toil in the rarefied air, with throbbing hearts and panting lungs, we reached the top of the gorge and squeezed ourselves between two gigantic fragments of rock by a passage called the "Dog's Lift," when I climbed on the shoulders of one man and then was hauled up. This introduced us by an abrupt turn round the southwest angle of the Peak to a narrow shelf of considerable length, rugged, uneven, and so overhung by the cliff in some places that it is necessary to crouch to pass at all. Above, the Peak looks nearly vertical for 400 feet; and below, the most tremendous precipice I have ever seen descends in one unbroken fall. This is usually considered the most dangerous part of the ascent, but it does not seem so to me, for such foothold as there is is secure, and one fancies that it is possible to hold on with the hands. But there, and on the final, and, to my thinking, the worst part of the climb, one slip, and a breathing, thinking, human being would lie 3,000 feet below, a shapeless, bloody heap!

—ISABELLA BIRD,
A Lady's Life in the Rocky Mountains (1881)

A CHANCE ENCOUNTER

*I*T WAS ONE OF THOSE UNEXPECTED FEASTS OF THE spirit—one that can only be stumbled upon. While driving in Wales, I noticed a small sign for an unfamiliar place, Wyre Park, tilted awkwardly in the direction of a large grove of trees. Parking the car and wandering toward the grove, I realized the leaves had suddenly changed, now damp and wind-tossed. Hearing water rushing nearby, I followed the sound and came upon a glorious waterfall. Not a large one, but one that left me in awe. Walking off to the right along a wood path, I found another world, one in which I wanted to get lost for days and days and days.

—LISA BACH, "A WALK IN WALES"

December 30

STAY AWHILE

*T*HIS WAS THE MOMENT I LONGED FOR EVERY day. Settling at a heavy inn-table, thawing and tingling, with wine, bread, and cheese handy and my papers, books and diary all laid out; writing up the day's doings, hunting for words in the dictionary, drawing, struggling with verses, or merely subsiding in a vacuous and contented trance while the snow thawed off my boots. An elderly woman came downstairs and settled by the stove with her sewing. Spotting my stick and rucksack and the puddle of melting snow, she said, with a smile, *"Wer reitet so spät durch Nacht und Wind?"* My German, now fifteen days old, was just up to this: "Who rides so late through night and wind?" I knew what to say at this point, and came in on cue. *"Englischer Student…zu Fuss nach Konstantiopel"* [hiking to Constantinople] I'd got it pat by now. "Konstantinopel?" she said. "Oh Weh!" O Woe! So far! And in midwinter too. She asked where I would be the day after, on New Year's Eve. Somewhere on the road, I said. "You can't go wandering about in the snow on Sylvesterabend!" she answered. "And where are you staying tonight, pray?" I hadn't thought yet. Her husband had come in a little while before and overheard our exchange. "Stay with us," he said. "You must be our guest."

—PATRICK LEIGH FERMOR, *A Time of Gifts*

A PRAYER FOR THE NEW YEAR

*I*T WAS NEW YEAR'S EVE. I WAS GOING TO GO TO THE beach at midnight, like most of the residents of Copacabana and Ipanema, who, dressed in white, congregate to light a candle in the sand and throw a white flower into the ocean with a prayer for the goddess Iemanjá. I asked my friend Doña Jurema how I should pray.

"I would say something like this," she began. "Iemanjá, Our Mother, please make this year a better year than the last. Not that last year was a bad year, don't get me wrong: I received many benefits, many good things happened to me, and I'm not complaining. But now, thinking over everything that's happened, I would like to ask you for something from the bottom of my heart: please bring me twice the amount of good things, and take away half the number of bad."

—ALMA GUILLERMOPRIETO, *Samba*

ACKNOWLEDGMENTS

I'd like to recognize the passionate travelers who helped me on my journey to publish *365 Travel*. To the gang at Travelers' Tales—Larry, James, Wenda, Susan, Jennifer, Tanya, Tara, Deborah, Kathy, Sean, and Krista—thank you for everything. Your dedication is remarkable, and your friendship enduring. I am grateful to Michele Wetherbee and Melanie Haage for their talent and design savvy. I'd also like to acknowledge the many talented travel writers whom I've worked with over the years, especially Brad Newsham, Laurie Gough, Marybeth Bond, Pamela Michael, Allen Noren, and Mikkel Aaland. Travel writers are the greatest people you'll ever have the pleasure of encountering, whether at home or on the road.

Of course no acknowledgments are complete without thanking those close to you for their love, encouragement, humor, and friendship. Thanks to: my family—Barbara (Mom), William (Dad), David, Laura, Amy, Steve, and the little ones: Joshua, Jacob, Daniel, Jessica, Aaron, and Noah; my extended family—Stacy, Penni, and Jane; my amazing friends—Kim Arnone, Kevin Bentley, Andrea Bourguet, Jeff Campbell, Leisha Fry, Phil Hahn, Laura Harger, Robin Helbling, Daniel Jason, Karen Levine, Rachel Longan, Jennifer Nannini, Gena Rickon, Inge Schilperoord, Erica Smith, Tacy Trowbridge, Deanna Quinones, and Beth Weber.

And to my travel companion for life, Kara Thacker—what a heavenly trip we're on, 365 days a year.

I Wonder as I Wander by Langston Hughes published by Farrar, Straus & Giroux, LLC. Copyright © 1956 by Langston Hughes, renewed 1984 by George Houston Bass.

Nothing to Declare: Memoirs of a Woman Traveling Alone by Marry Morris published by Houghton Mifflin. Copyright © 1988 by Mary Morris.

Video Night in Kathmandu by Pico Iyer published by Vintage Books, a division of Random House, Inc. Copyright © 1988 by Pico Iyer.

Under the Tuscan Sun by Frances Mayes published by Chronicle Books. Copyright © 1996 by Frances Mayes.

Introduction by Phil Cousineau excerpted from *Pilgrimage: Adventures of the Spirit,* edited by Sean O'Reilly and James O'Reilly, published by Travelers' Tales. Copyright © 2000 by Travelers' Tales, Inc.

Fresh Air Fiend: Travel Writings by Paul Theroux published by Houghton Mifflin. Copyright © 2000 by Paul Theroux.

The Italian Hours by Henry James originally published in 1909.

Walden by Henry David Thoreau originally published in 1854 by Ticknor and Fields.

America Day by Day by Simone de Beauvoir published by Orion House. Copyright © 1954 by Simone de Beauvoir.

Letter to her family by Gertrude Bell written in 1917.

Lost in Place: Growing Up Absurd in Suburbia by Mark Salzman published by Random House. Copyright © 1995 by Mark Salzman.

The Road from the Past: Traveling through History in France by Ina Caro published by Nan A. Talese, an imprint of Bantam Doubleday Dell. Copyright © 1994 by Ina Caro.

More Tramps Abroad by Mark Twain originally published in 1897 by Chatto and Windus.

"A Simple Touch" by Robert J. Matthews excerpted from *The Gift of Travel,* edited by Larry Habegger, James O'Reilly, and Sean O'Reilly, published by Travelers' Tales. Copyright © 1997 by Robert J. Matthews. Reprinted by permission of the author.

A Negro Explorer at the North Pole by Matthew A. Henson originally published in 1912 by Frederick A. Stokes Company.

Behind the Wall by Colin Thubron published by Atlantic Monthly Press. Copyright © 1987 by Colin Thubron.

Magic and Mystery in Tibet by Alexandra David-Neel originally published in 1931 by Bodley Head, a division of Random House, Inc.

The Way of the Wanderer by David Yeadon published by Travelers' Tales. Copyright © 2000 by David Yeadon.

At Home and Abroad by V. S. Prichett published by North Point Press, a division of Farrar, Strauss & Giroux, LLC. Copyright © 1989 by V. S. Prichett.

Pole to Pole: North to South by Camel, River Raft, and Balloon by Michael Palin published by BBC Books. Copyright © 1992 by Michael Palin.

Narrative of the U.S. Exploring Expedition by Authority of Congress during the Years 1838-1842 by Charles Wilkes published in 1843.

The Royal Road to Romance by Richard Halliburton published by Travelers' Tales. Copyright © 1925 by Richard Halliburton.

Bitter Lemons by Laurence Durrell published by E. P. Dutton, a division of Penguin Putnam Inc. Copyright © 1957 by Laurence Durrell.

"Traveling Light" by Bunny McBride published with permission from the author. Copyright © 2001 by Bunny McBride.

"Just My Imagination" by Christine Nielsen published with permission from the author. Copyright © 2001 by Christine Nielsen.

A Long Way from St. Louie by Colleen J. McElroy published by Coffee House Press. Copyright © 1997 by Colleen J. McElroy.

Serpent in Paradise by Dea Birkett published by Doubleday, a division of Random House, Inc. Copyright © 1998 by Dea Birkett.

From Cape to Cairo: An African Odyssey by David Ewing Duncan published by Weidenfeld & Nicolson. Copyright © 1989 by David Ewing Duncan.

Endurance by Alfred Lansing originally published by McGraw Hill. Copyright © 1959 by Alfred Lansing.

The Wind in My Wheels by Josie Dew published by Little, Brown & Co., UK. Copyright © 1992 by Josie Dew.

My Early Life by Sir Winston Churchill originally published in 1930 by Thornton Butterworth.

Take Me With You: A Round-the-World Journey to Invite a Stranger Home by Brad Newsham published by Travelers' Tales. Copyright © 2000 by Brad Newsham.

Letters from Gourgounel by Kenneth White copyright © 1986.

"Fearless in France" by Margo Hacket published with permission from the author. Copyright © 2000 by Margo Hacket.

A Portrait of All the Russias by Laurens van der Post published by William Morrow & Co., a division of HarperCollins Publishers, Inc. Copyright © 1964 by Laurens van der Post.

The South Seas Dream: An Adventure in Paradise by John Dyson published by Little, Brown, & Co. Copyright © 1982 by John Dyson.

Six Months in the Sandwich Islands by Isabella Bird originally published in 1873 by John Murray.

The Brazilian Sound: Samba, Bossa Nova, and the Popular Music of Brazil by Chris McGowan and Ricardo Pessanha published by Temple University Press. Copyright © 1998 by Chris McGowan and Ricardo Pessanha.

Road Scholar: Coast to Coast Late in the Century by Andrei Codrescu published by Hyperion, a division of Disney Book Publishing Inc. Copyright © 1993 by Andrei Codrescu. Reprinted by permission.

How to Travel: Hints, Advice, and Suggestions to Travelers by Land and Sea All Over the Globe by Thomas W. Knox originally published in 1881.

"Yearning for Faraway Places" by Sophia Dembling published with permission from the author. Copyright © 2001 by Sophia Dembling.

An Area of Darkness by V. S. Naipaul published by Vintage Books, a division of Random House, Inc. Copyright © 1964 by V. S. Naipaul.

South America by James Bryce published in 1912 by Macmillan Company.

The Complete Book of Marvels by Richard Halliburton published by Bobbs-Merrill. Copyright © 1941 by Richard Halliburton.

"North" by Mary Hussman published with permission from the author. Copyright © 2000 by Mary Hussman.

The Road to Oxiana by Robert Byron originally published in 1937 by Jonathan Cape Ltd., a division of Random House, UK. Copyright © 1937 by Robert Byron.

The Ladder of St. Augustine by H. W. Longfellow originally published in 1850.

Journal...During the Voyage...of H.M.S. Beagle, 1832-36 by Charles Darwin originally published in 1936.

Paris was Yesterday by Janet Flanner published by Viking, a division of Penguin Putnam, Inc. Copyright © 1972 by Janet Flanner.

Traveling Light by Bill Barich published by Viking, a division of Penguin Putnam, Inc. Copyright © 1981 by Bill Barich.

Letter by Gertrude Bell written in 1898.

One's Company by Peter Fleming originally published in 1937 by Jonathan Cape, a division of Random House, UK. Copyright © 1937 by Peter Fleming.

Mornings in Mexico by D. H. Lawrence originally published in 1927 by Alfred A. Knopf, a division of Random House, Inc. Copyright © 1927 by D. H. Lawrence.

A Persian Journey: Being an Etcher's Impression of the Middle East by Fred Richards originally published in 1932 by Jonathan Cape/Harrison Smith.

"A Woman's Path" by Sally Lowe Whitehead published with permission from the author. Copyright © 2001 by Sally Lowe Whitehead.

A Trip to the Light Fantastic: Travels with a Mexican Circus by Katie Hickman published by Flamingo. Copyright © 1995 by Katie Hickman.

The Pedro Gorino by Harry Dean originally published in 1929 by Houghton Mifflin. Copyright © 1929 by Harry Dean.

"Lost and Found" by Joel Simon excerpted from *Travelers' Tales India*, edited by James O'Reilly and Larry Habegger, published by Travelers' Tales. Copyright © 1994 by Joel Simon. Reprinted by permission of the author.

Encore Provence: New Adventures in the South of France by Peter Mayle published by Alfred A. Knopf, a division of Random House, Inc. Copyright © 1999 by Peter Mayle.

"Longing" by Neise Cavini Turchin excerpted from *Travelers' Tales Brazil*, edited by Scott Doggett and Annette Haddad, published by Travelers' Tales. Copyright © 1997 by Neise Cavini Turchin. Reprinted by permission of the author.

My Love Affair with England by Susan Allen Toth published by Ballantine, a division of Random House, Inc. Copyright © 1992 by Susan Allen Toth.

Sunny Memories of Foreign Lands by Harriet Beecher Stowe originally published in 1854.

From Sea to Sea by Rudyard Kipling originally published in 1897.

Look a Lion in the Eye: On Safari through Africa by Kathryn Hulme published by Atlantic Monthly Press. Copyright © 1974 by Kathryn Hulme.

"Buddha is Italian" by Eric Lurio excerpted from *Travelers' Tales Nepal*, edited by Rajendra S. Khadka, published by Travelers' Tales. Copyright © 1997 by Eric Lurio. Reprinted by permission of the author.

"In Connemara" by Sara Fraser published with permission from the author. Copyright © 2001 by Sara Fraser.

Denmark Is a Lovely Land by Hudson Strode published by Harcourt Brace. Copyright © 1951 by Hudson Strode.

Alexander's Path by Freya Stark published by Harcourt Brace. Copyright © 1958 by Freya Stark.

In an Antique Land: History in the Guise of a Traveler's Tales by Amitav Ghoosh published by Vintage Books, a division of Random House. Copyright © 1992 by Amitav Ghoosh.

373

The Snow Leopard by Peter Matthiessen published by Viking, a division of Penguin Putnam, Inc. Copyright © 1978 by Peter Matthiessen.

Natural Opium: Some Travelers' Tales by Diane Johnson published by Alfred A. Knopf, a division of Random House, Inc. Copyright © 1992 by Diane Johnson.

"In Salamanca" by James O'Reilly excerpted from *Travelers' Tales Spain,* edited by Lucy McCauley, published by Travelers' Tales. Copyright © 1995 by James O'Reilly. Reprinted by permission of the author.

Nothing to Declare: Memoirs of a Woman Traveling Alone by Mary Morris published by Houghton Mifflin. Copyright © 1988 by Mary Morris.

Brazil Up Close: The Sensual and Adventurous Guide by Pamela Bloom published by Hunter Publications. Copyright © 1996 by Pamela Bloom.

"Vagabond" by Carol Levy excerpted from *Travelers' Tales India,* edited by James O'Reilly and Larry Habegger, published by Travelers' Tales. Copyright © 1994 by Carol Levy. Reprinted by permission of the author.

"Paradise" by Suzanne McFayden-Smith published with permission from the author. Copyright © 2001 by Suzanne McFayden-Smith.

To Jerusalem and Back: A Personal Account by Saul Bellow published by Viking Press, a division of Penguin Putnam, Inc. Copyright © 1976 by Saul Bellow.

Paddle to the Amazon: The Ultimate 12,000 Mile Canoe Adventure by Don Starkell published by Prima Publishing. Copyright © 1989 by Don Starkell.

The Back of Beyond: Travels to the Wild Places of the Earth by David Yeadon published with HarperCollins Publishers, Inc. Copyright © 1991 by David Yeadon.

"Why We Travel," by Pico Iyer appeared in Salon.com at http://www.salon.com. Copyright © 2000 by Pico Iyer.

Jaguars Ripped My Flesh by Tim Cahill published by Bantam Books, a division of Random House, Inc. Copyright © 1987 by Tim Cahill.

More Tramps Abroad by Mark Twain originally published in 1897.

Incidents of Travel in Egypt by John Lloyd Stephens originally published in 1837.

Grand and Private Pleasures by Caskie Stinnett published by Atlantic Monthly Press. Copyright © 1969, 1977 by Caskie Stinnett.

"Walking to Santiago" by William Dalrymple originally appeared in the August 1992 issue of *Condé Nast Traveler.* Copyright © 1992 by William Dalrymple.

Diary by Virginia Woolf published by Harcourt Brace. Copyright © 1979 by Virginia Woolf.

ACKNOWLEDGMENTS

A Natural History of Love by Diane Ackerman published by Vintage Books, a division of Random House, Inc. Copyright © 1994 by Diane Ackerman.

A Journey of One's Own: Uncommon Advice for the Independent Woman Traveler by Thalia Zepatos published by Eighth Mountain Press. Copyright © 1992 by Thalia Zepatos.

Shooting the Boh by Tracy Johnston published by Vintage Books, a division of Random House, Inc. Copyright © 1992 by Tracy Johnston.

Sahara Unveiled: A Journey Across the Desert by William Langewiesche published by Vintage Books, a division of Random House, Inc. Copyright © 1996 by William Langewiesche.

In an Enchanted Island by W. H. Mallock originally published in 1889.

A Lady's Life in the Rocky Mountains by Isabella Bird originally published in 1881.

Introduction by Robert Hass excerpted from *The Gift of Rivers*, edited by Pamela Michael, published by Travelers' Tales. Copyright © 1999 by Travelers' Tales.

First Over Everest! The Houston-Mount Everest Expedition by Colonel P. T. Etherton, et. al. originally published in 1933 by Robert McBride & Co.

Letter by Freya Stark written June 18, 1938.

"Kona Dreamtime" by James O'Reilly excerpted from *Travelers' Tales Hawai'i*, edited by Rick and Marcie Carroll, published by Travelers' Tales. Copyright © 1999 by James O'Reilly.

Wall to Wall: From Beijing to Berlin by Rail by Mary Morris published by Penguin Putnam, Inc. Copyright © 1991 by Mary Morris.

"Rhythms of Japan" by Kara Thacker published with permission from the author. Copyright © 2001 by Kara Thacker.

"In Love with Scotland" by Kara Knafelc published with permission from the author. Copyright © 2001 by Kara Knafelc.

A Book of Migrations by Rebecca Solnit published by Verso. Copyright © 1997 by Rebecca Solnit.

Geography and Plays by Gertrude Stein originally published in 1922 by Four Seas.

"The Soul of an Intercontinental Wanderer" by Pico Iyer originally appeared in the April 1993 issue of *Harper's* magazine. Copyright © 1993 by Pico Iyer.

Mountaineering in the Land of the Midnight Sun by Mrs. Aubrey LeBlond originally published in 1908 by J. B. Lippincott Co.

Saturday Night in Baoding: A China Memoir by Richard Terrill published by University of Arkansas Press. Copyright © 1990 by Richard Terrill.

The Innocents Abroad by Mark Twain originally published in 1869.

Travelers' Tales Nepal edited by Rajendra S. Khadka, published by Travelers' Tales. Copyright © 1998 by Travelers' Tales.

"At the Baths" by Laura Fraser published with permission from the author. Copyright © 2001 by Laura Fraser.

"Sueños" by Cristine Del Sol excerpted from *Travelers' Tales Spain,* edited by Lucy McCauley, published by Travelers' Tales. Copyright © 1995 by Cristine Del Sol. Reprinted by permission of the author.

"Irish Memories" by Mireya Morales Quirie published with permission from the author. Copyright © 2001 by Mireya Morales Quirie.

Gift from the Sea by Anne Morrow Lindbergh published by Pantheon Books, a division of Random House, Inc. Copyright © 1955 by Anne Morrow Lindbergh.

Personal Narrative of a Pilgrimage to Al-Madinah and Meccah by Sir Richard Burton originally published in 18555-56 by Longman & Co.

At Home and Abroad: Things and Thoughts in America and Europe by Margaret Fuller Ossoli originally published in 1848 by Roberts Brothers.

Sea and Sardinia by D. H. Lawrence originally published in 1921.

How to Travel: Hints, Advice, and Suggestions to Travelers by Land and Sea All Over the Globe by Thomas W. Knox originally published in 1881.

Letter to His Mother by Robert Louis Stevenson originally published in 1872.

"Bach in Brazil" by Phil Cousineau published with permission from the author. Copyright © 2001 by Phil Cousineau.

Holiday Magazine excerpt by Ernest Hemingway originally appeared in the July 1949 issue.

Travels by Jan Morris published by Harcourt Brace Jovanovich. Copyright © 1976 by Jan Morris.

Arabian Sands by Wilfred Thesiger published by Penguin Putnam, Inc. Copyright © 1959, 1984, 1991 by Wilfred Thesiger.

Backsheesh: A Woman's Wanderings by Mrs. William Beckman originally published in 1900.

Homage to Barcelona by Colm Tóibín published by Simon & Schuster. Copyright © 1990 by Colm Tóibín.

"Oh to Be in Paris" by Peter Mayle appeared in Salon.com at http://www.salon.com. Copyright © 1997 by Peter Mayle.

Land without Justice by Milovan Djilas published by Harcourt Brace Jovanovich. Copyright © 1958 by Milovan Djilas.

Downhill All the Way by Leonard Woolf published by Harcourt Brace. Copyright © 1967 by Leonard Woolf.

Letters from Syria (1927–1928) by Freya Stark published by John Murray. Copyright © 1942 by Freya Stark.

Take Me With You: An Around-the-World Journey to Bring a Stranger Home by Brad Newsham published by Travelers' Tales. Copyright © 2000 by Brad Newsham.

Slowly Down the Ganges by Eric Newby published by Hodder & Stoughton. Copyright © 1966 by Eric Newby.

"Fiddlin' Around" by Linda Watanabe McFerrin excerpted from *Travelers' Tales Ireland*, edited by James O'Reilly, Larry Habegger, and Sean O'Reilly, published by Travelers' Tales. Copyright © 2000 by Linda Watanabe McFerrin.

Nothing to Declare: Memoirs of a Woman Traveling Alone by Mary Morris published by Houghton Mifflin. Copyright © 1988 by Mary Morris.

Passenger to Tehran by Vita Sackville-West originally published in 1926.

South America by James Bryce originally published in 1912.

Narrative of a Voyage by Abby Jane Morrell originally published in 1833.

"Polite Persistence" by David Kravitz published with permission from the author. Copyright © 2001 by David Kravitz.

Travels in West Africa by Mary Kingsley originally published in 1897.

"Touching Improves a Vacation" by Blythe Foote Finke excerpted from *Travelers Tales Spain*, edited by Lucy McCauley, published by Travelers' Tales. Copyright © 1997 by Blythe Foote Finke. Reprinted by permission of the author.

"Imbrication" by Rebecca Lawton published with permission from the author. Copyright © 2001 by Rebecca Lawton.

"An Unladylike Journey" by Christine Weeber excerpted from *Solo: Her Own Journey*, edited by Susan Fox Rogers, published by Seal Press. Copyright © 1996 by Christine Weeber.

"On the Bus" by Tara Austen Weaver published with permission from the author. Copyright © 2001 by Tara Austen Weaver.

Tremendous Trifles by G. K. Chesterton originally published in 1909.

Vagabonding in the USA: A Guide for Independent Travelers and Foreign Visitors by Ed Buryn published by Ronin Publishing. Copyright © 1980 by Ed Buryn.

ACKNOWLEDGMENTS

Letter to Mr. Boyd by Elizabeth Barrett Browning originally published in 1847.

If I Had My Life to Live Over Again by Nadine Stair published by Paper-Mache Press. Copyright © 1992 by Nadine Stair.

A Time of Gifts by Patrick Leigh Fermor published by John Murray Ltd. Copyright © 1977 by Patrick Leigh Fermor.

Nellie Bly's Book: Around the World in Seventy-Two Days by Elizbeth Cochrane Seaman originally published in 1890.

Diary by Lewis Carroll originally published in 1867.

Journal by Dorothy Wordsworth originally published in 1803.

Who Is the River: Getting Lost in the Amazon and Other Places by Paul Zalis published by Simon & Schuster, Inc. Copyright © 1986 by Paul Zalis.

English Traits by Ralph Waldo Emerson originally published in 1856.

"High Society" by Ann Jones published with permission from the author. Copyright © 2001 by Ann Jones.

Journey without Maps by Graham Greene originally published in 1936.

"Getaway" by Susan Brady published with permission from the author. Copyright © 2001 by Susan Brady.

The Road from the Past: Traveling through History in France by Ina Caro published by Nan A. Talese, an imprint of Bantam Doubleday Dell. Copyright © 1994 by Ina Caro.

Diary by Virginia Woolf published by Harcourt Brace. Copyright © 1979 by Virginia Woolf.

"Road Trip" by Lisa Bach published with permission from the author. Copyright © 2001 by Lisa Bach.

First Over Everest!: The Houston-Mount Everest Expedition by Colonel P. T. Etherton, et al. originally published in 1933 by Robert McBride.

Kite Strings of the Southern Cross: A Woman's Travel Odyssey by Laurie Gough published by Travelers' Tales (U.S.) and Turnstone Press (Canada). Copyright © 1999 by Laurie Gough. Published by permission.

The Attentive Heart: Conversations with Trees by Stephanie Kaza published by Fawcett Columbine, a division of Random House, Inc. Copyright © 1993 by Stephanie Kaza.

"Room Checking" by Peter Davis excerpted from *Not So Funny When It Happened,* edited by Tim Cahill, published by Travelers' Tales. Copyright © 2000 by Peter Davis.

Dwellings: A Spiritual History of the Living World by Linda Hogan published by W. W. Norton and Company. Copyright © 1995 by Linda Hogan.

Letter to the Earl of Strafford by Horace Walpole originally published in 1769.

The Story of My Life by Helen Keller originally published in 1928 by Houghton Mifflin.

Storm: A Motorcycle Journey of Love, Endurance, and Transformation by Allen Noren published by Travelers' Tales. Copyright © 2000 by Allen Noren.

Travelling Alone: A Woman's Journey Round the World by Lilian Leland originally published in 1890.

Hitchhiking Vietnam: A Woman's Solo Journey in an Elusive Land by Karin Muller published by Globe Pequot. Copyright © 1998 by Karin Muller.

Legends of the American Desert: Sojourns in the Greater Southwest by Alex Shoumatoff published by Alfred A. Knopf, a division of Random House. Copyright © 1997 by Alex Shoumatoff.

The Name of Things by Susan Brind Morrow published by Riverhead Books, a division of Penguin Putnam, Inc. Copyright © 1997 by Susan Brind Morrow.

"Lady of the Avenues" by Sean O'Reilly excerpted from *Travelers' Tales San Francisco*, edited by James O'Reilly, Larry Habegger and Sean O'Reilly, published by Travelers' Tales. Copyright © 1996 by Sean O'Reilly.

Spanish Pilgrimage: A Canter to St. James by Robin Hanbury-Tenison published by Random House, UK. Copyright © 1990 by Robin Hanbury-Tenison.

Life on the Mississippi by Mark Twain originally published in 1883.

Letter to Count D'Orsay by Charles Dickens originally published in 1844.

Native Stranger: A Black American's Journey into the Heart of Africa by Eddy L. Harris published by Simon & Schuster. Copyright © 1992 by Eddy L. Harris.

Interview with Colonel Jimmy Roberts excerpted from *Travelers' Tales Nepal*, edited by Rajendra S. Khadka, published by Travelers' Tales. Copyright © 1997 by Colonel Jimmy Roberts.

"Groping Italian Men" by Kristen Nesbitt published with permission from the author. Copyright © 2001 by Kristen Nesbitt.

"Enchanted" by Cheryl Bentley excerpted from *Travelers' Tales India*, edited by James O'Reilly and Larry Habegger, published by Travelers' Tales. Copyright © 1995 by Cheryl Bentley.

Ladies on the Loose by Leo Hamalian published by Dodd, Mead & Co. Copyright © 1981 by Leo Hamalian.

The Alhambra by Washington Irving originally published in 1832.

Backsheesh: A Woman's Wanderings by Mrs. William Beckman originally published in 1900.

Don't Mention the War! by Stewart Ferris and Paul Bassett published by Summersdale Publishers Ltd. Copyright © 1998 by Stewart Ferris and Paul Bassett.

West with the Night by Beryl Markham published by North Point Press, a division of Farrar, Strauss & Giroux, LLC. Copyright © 1942 by Beryl Markham.

"Finding Myself in the World" by Dorothy Lazard excerpted from *Go Girl*, edited by Elaine Lee, published by Eighth Mountain Press. Copyright © 1997 by Dorothy Lazard.

Sacred Monkey River: A Canoe Trip with the Gods by Christopher Shaw published by W. W. Norton. Copyright © 2000 by Christopher Shaw.

An English Woman in America by Isabella Bird originally published in 1856.

The Sword of Heaven: A Five Continent Odyssey to Save the World by Mikkel Aaland published by Travelers' Tales. Copyright © 1999 by Mikkel Aaland.

Michelle Dominique Leigh excerpted from *The House on Via Gombito: Writing by American Women,* edited by C. W. Truesdale and Madelon Sprengnether, published by New Rivers Press. Copyright © 1997 by Michelle Dominique Leigh.

Harper's Handbook for Travelers by W. Pembroke Fetridge originally published in 1862.

Wanderlust: Overland Through Asia and Africa by Dan Spitzer published by Richard Marek Publishers. Copyright © 1979 by Dan Spitzer.

Beaten Paths, or a Woman's Vacation by Ella W. Thompson originally published in 1874 by Lee & Shepard.

"Baksheesh" by Keith Kellett excerpted from *Not So Funny When It Happened,* edited by Tim Cahill, published by Travelers' Tales. Copyright © 2000 by Keith Kellett. Reprinted by permission of the author.

The Happy Traveller: A Book for Poor Men by Frank Tatchell originally published in 1923.

Alone by Admiral Richard E. Byrd originally published in 1938 by G. P. Putnum's Sons.

Cities by Arthur Symons originally published in 1903.

Round the World in Any Number of Days by Maurice Baring originally published in 1913.

ACKNOWLEDGMENTS

Running North: A Yukon Adventure by Ann Mariah Cook published by Algonquin Books. Copyright © 1998 by Ann Mariah Cook. Reprinted by permission of Algonquin Books of Chapel Hill, a division of Workman Publishing.

African Nights by Kuki Gallmann published by HarperCollins Publishers, Inc. Copyright © 1994 by Kuki Gallmann.

The Desert and the Sown by Gertrude Bell originally published in 1905.

"San Sebastian" by Judy Rose excerpted from *Love & Romance*, edited by Judy Babcock Wylie, published by Travelers' Tales. Copyright © 1998 by Judy Rose. Published by permission of the author.

The Royal Road to Romance by Richard Halliburton published by Travelers' Tales. Copyright © 1925 by Richard Halliburton.

The Road to Oxiana by Robert Byron originally published in 1937 by Jonathan Cape Ltd., a division of Random House, UK. Copyright © 1937 by Robert Byron.

The Back of Beyond: Travels to the Wild Places of the Earth by David Yeadon published by HarperCollins Publishers, Inc. Copyright © 1991 by David Yeadon.

"Waiting for the Eclipse" by Natanya Pearlman published with permission from the author. Copyright © 2001 by Natanya Pearlman.

Catfish and Mandala by Andrew X. Pham published by Farrar, Strauss & Giroux, LLC. Copyright © 1999 by Andrew X. Pham.

The Isle of Shamrock by Clifton Johnson originally published in 1901.

Georgiana Goddard King excerpted from *Heart of Spain*, edited by Agnes Morgan, published by Harvard University Press. Copyright © 1942.

"A World Below" by Jennifer Leo published with permission from the author. Copyright © 2001 by Jennfer Leo.

Cities of Sicily by Edward Hutton originally published in 1925 by Little Brown & Co. Copyright © 1925 by Edward Hutton.

Incidents of Travel in Egypt by John Lloyd Stephens originally published in 1837.

"The Valley of Refuge" by Mary Orr excerpted from *Travelers' Tales India*, edited by James O'Reilly and Larry Habegger, published by Travelers' Tales. Copyright © 1995 by Mary Orr.

How Deep the High Journey by Margaret Stark copyright © 1997 by Margaret Stark.

"Bird of the Desert" by David Roberts published with permission from the author. Copyright © 2001 by David Roberts.

"Touring Spain" by Lucy McCauley published with permission from the author. Copyright © 2001 by Lucy McCauley.

Pleasures of a Tangled Life by Jan Morris published by Random House, Inc. Copyright © 1989 by Jan Morris.

A Little Tour in France by Henry James originally published in 1882.

"Why We Travel," by Pico Iyer appeared in Salon.com at http://www.salon.com. Copyright © 2000 by Pico Iyer.

Nellie Bly's Book: Around the World in Seventy-Two Days by Elizabeth Cochrane Seaman originally published in 1890.

The Royal Road to Romance by Richard Halliburton published by Travelers' Tales. Copyright © 1925 by Richard Halliburton.

"The Carlsbad Caverns" by Padma Jayaraj published with permission from the author. Copyright © 2001 by Padma Jayaraj.

"Hitchhiking Iceland" by Q Williams published with permission from the author. Copyright © 2001 by Q Williams.

Italy: The Places In Between by Kate Simon published by HarperCollins Publishers, Inc. Copyright © 1970 by Kate Simon.

"Inside the Map" by Laura Harger published with permission from the author. Copyright © 2001 by Laura Harger.

More Caviar by Art Buchwald published by HarperCollins Publishers, Inc. Copyright © 1958 by Art Buchwald.

Journal by Dorothy Wordsworth originally published in 1803.

"Strolling to Sikkim" by Larry Habegger excerpted from *Travelers' Tales India*, edited by James O'Reilly and Larry Habegger, published by Travelers' Tales. Copyright © 1995 by Larry Habegger.

Diary by Virginia Woolf published by Harcourt Brace. Copyright © 1979 by Virginia Woolf.

"Italian Awakenings" by Erica Smith published with permission from the author. Copyright © 2001 by Erica Smith.

Tell My Horse: Voodoo and Life in Haiti and Jamaica by Zora Neale Hurston published by HarperCollins Publishers, Inc. Copyright © 1928, 1996 by Zora Neale Hurston.

Letters from America by Rupert Brooke originally published in 1916 by Charles Scribner's Sons.

"Travels through Central America" by Brendan Powell published with permission from the author. Copyright © 2001 by Brendan Powell.

Journey to Kars by Philip Glazebrook published by Atheneum, a division of Simon & Schuster, Inc. Copyright © 1984 by Philip Glazebrook.

ABOUT THE EDITOR

LISA BACH is a freelance writer and editor with a Master's Degree in literature and more than ten years experience in book publishing. She has traveled to more than twenty countries, but having just bought a new home in Oakland, California, she will be spending more time with her luggage unpacked, reading and writing in front of her very own fireplace.